Critical Storytelling from behind Invisible Bars

Critical Storytelling

VOLUME 4

The titles published in this series are listed at *brill.com/csto*

Critical Storytelling from behind Invisible Bars

Undergraduates and Inmates Write Their Way Out

Edited by

Carmella J. Braniger, Alex V. Miller, Kathryn A. Coffey and
Rebekah M. Icenesse

BRILL

SENSE

LEIDEN | BOSTON

All chapters in this book have undergone peer review.

The Library of Congress Cataloging-in-Publication Data is available online at http://catalog.loc.gov

Typeface for the Latin, Greek, and Cyrillic scripts: "Brill". See and download: brill.com/brill-typeface.

ISSN 2590-0099
ISBN 978-90-04-44164-4 (paperback)
ISBN 978-90-04-44163-7 (hardback)
ISBN 978-90-04-44165-1 (e-book)

For Greg
With love
— CJB

• • •

For my parents
You taught me how to be strong and have always supported my dreams
I am thankful for everything you do for me
— RMI

• • •

For my family and friends near and far
In memory of my Nana and Poppy
You have been there always, and I'll always be grateful for it
— KAC

• • •

For Angela, my perfect love, and my parents, for showing the way
To all those who were patient, when they had no cause
— AVM

• •
•

Even in a prisoner's uniform, I've experienced a freedom very few people get the chance to.

SANDRA BROWN (#R-35900, Decatur Correctional Center)

• •
•

Contents

Preface

When we speak of social justice, we often talk about how victims—the down-trodden, marginalized, and disenfranchised—may be uplifted through collective social change. Not many, though, recognize the need to provide such encouragement to prison inmates, especially female inmates. Imprisoned women are some of the most vulnerable members of society. Incarceration strips away their identity. Disempowering and objectifying them, the institution gives these women a number and uniform to reinforce their separation from society. Once given the chance to reintegrate, former inmates often struggle to elude the label they have been given, making it challenging to change their lives. Forever and always, they are known as offenders.

Prison writing has always been seen as a form of political resistance. From Jack London to Malcolm X to Jack Henry Abbott, male writers have dominated the history of the prison narrative. Silenced female inmate voices need to be heard and contextualized within the larger metanarrative of prison literature. We need more critical projects to examine, expose, analyze, as well as challenge deeply-entrenched narratives and characterizations of incarcerated women, whose histories are often marked by sexual abuse, domestic violence, poverty, PTSD, a lack of education, housing insecurity, mental illness, and substance abuse and addiction. In a response to the need for more female inmates' voices, Millikin University and the Decatur Correctional Center provided female inmates of the center the opportunity to voice their histories, which often counter dominant incarceration narratives. The DCC women were asked, along with undergraduate cohorts, to tell their critical stories from behind visible and invisible bars.

Storytelling, when it's critical, is inclusive. It doubts common sense. It questions the *status quo*. It tears down regimes of domination. It envisions possibilities for change. Critical storytellers voice silences, and rely on diverse storytelling methods, theoretical approaches, and narrative frameworks to offer new stories that are critical of exclusionary and divisive metanarratives. Critical storytelling fights what Paulo Freire refers to in his landmark 1970 book *Pedagogy of the Oppressed* as "naïve consciousness" and, instead, raises critical and political awareness. Critical stories are counternarratives that focus on a moment of personal transformation, but subjective experiences do not operate in a vacuum. Such qualitative inquiry can show us a slice of the lives of authors who are brave enough to write their stories.

So what does it mean to write from behind physical and metaphorical bars, some of which are visible, or tangible, while others remain invisible, below the surface, buried deep in our subconscious? Prison contains invisible cages within itself. Sure, the physical part of being locked up is hard but equally debilitating is having your voice shackled, your dreams thrown away, and your right to express feelings withheld. The invisible prison of doubt about one's place in the free world overshadows every thought.

Several of the writers featured in this volume wrote the entire time they were incarcerated at the Decatur Correctional Center for Women in Decatur, IL. These women, all participants in Alex Miller's Shakespeare Corrected, wrote from the heart, even when it felt almost too painful. The pain did not come without some joy, and many incarcerates chose to write favorite memories. For example, in the story "Sentimental Syrup," published in this volume, Cara Quiett writes about her memories of cooking simple meals for her family. To help her through her days behind physical bars, she would attempt to relive those moments of freedom on paper. She says, "The escape was never long or real enough but it reminded me that I was happy and free with potential. So very long ago. And could I be again?"

Barriers don't always have to be physical; the metaphorical ones can do just as much damage. Invisible bars inhibit progress with insecurities and instances of self-doubt. Relaying struggle on paper isn't always easy for some people. As a writer and editor, Kathyrn confesses:

> At times, I didn't find it easy, because I still live with my anxiety and destructive habits, and in doing so, it made me worry about how others would see me. However, over time I realized that when it comes to coping with invisible bars, it helps to take it one day at a time.

Some days will be worse than others, but it's important to remember the small victories that can help you move forward. And one way to break down these invisible bars is to write your way to freedom. It may be the first step, but it's one for an amazing journey ahead.

When asked, Rebekah described what it was like to write and edit from behind *invisible* bars:

> I didn't realize what invisible bars were until I became a writer and editor for this book where I had to write behind those bars, my own invisible bars. Invisible bars are struggles that you are facing. It's like you're a prisoner in your own mind; only you can see the bars that are in front of you.

The bars we write about in this collection take the form of struggles, emotions, addictions, grief, or any demon one is trying to overcome. These bars can be painful, like you're grasping for freedom but can't be released from them yet.

It takes time. A lot of your time and energy. Time that you can't get back. You want to show the bars that have imprisoned you, so you write down your story.

Writing from behind these invisible bars means that you are telling your truth. Cara's further reflection on workshops with fellow inmates of the Decatur Correctional Center and Millikin students demonstrates the importance of such an opportunity for rendering her own truth:

> To hear the stories of other inmates was the first time I had felt a sisterhood and sense of trust from a group of strangers. I had done quite a few years with some of these girls. It was not that I did not like them. I just chose to keep to myself. Put my head down, shut up, and do my time. But to feel trust again, to share something deep and make myself vulnerable was actually freeing. Their stories were also all very interesting. I saw 'them.' The 'them' from before. The innocence they lost in the process of their journey. Dr. B and the students were also very helpful. They sincerely wanted to collaborate and get our stories out there. I felt interesting, and interested, again, as opposed to feeling judged. The students worked with us in person and via prison snail mail. It made me realize that we were not entirely forgotten. Maybe the rest of society that still has negative thoughts about inmates can somehow set aside their own prisons of judgement to read these essays and find connectivity within the pages.

The critical stories in this volume *Critical Storytelling from Behind Invisible Bars* will provoke readers to 'set aside their own prisons,' to acknowledge and question unquestioned norms and assumptions. These stories expose oppression in its various forms, from violence, sexism, racism, bullying, exploitation, and marginalization to dehumanization and cultural imperialism. These passionate narrators have the guts to think, act, and question, vulnerably. And their stories provide a space for marginalized, silenced community voices to seek external resonance and validation.

The authors of the personal stories you will find in this volume work to situate and contextualize personal subjectivities and transformations within the larger culture(s) of imprisonment. All authors in this volume write their way out of questionable and sometimes unbearable oppressive environments and search for hope for a better future for themselves and those whose lives they impact. Through telling their critical stories, incarcerated women at Decatur's Correctional Center and Millikin undergraduates work together to sustain recovery from trauma, make positive changes and informed decisions, create a real sense of empowerment, strengthen their capacity to exercise personal agency, and inspire audiences to create change far outside the reaches of prison walls.

Notes on Contributors

Editors

Carmella J. Braniger

is Associate Professor of English, at Millikin University where she teaches first-year writing, creative writing, literature, and classical rhetoric. Her poems have appeared in *Sycamore Review, Poems and Plays, The Dirty Napkin, MARGIE: The American Journal of Poetry, Modern English Tanka, Magnapoets, Atlas Poetica,* and many others. Pudding House Publications published her chapbook, *No One May Follow,* in 2009. Dr. Braniger co-authored a book chapter entitled "Redefining the Undergraduate English Writing Major: An Integrated Approach at a Small Comprehensive University" in the collection *What We Are Becoming: Developments in Undergraduate Writing Majors,* published by Utah State University Press. She was co-editor of *Critical Storytelling in Uncritical Times,* volume 2, published by Brill | Sense. Her critical story "'Hey, Sister': Utterances, Sexualities, and Dialectical Tensions in Sibling Relationships" also appeared in the same volume. She enjoys collaboratively writing and publishing poetry sequences and critical stories with fellow faculty and students.

Kathryn A. Coffey

has been wanting to write and share her own stories since pre-school. Literally, since pre-school. She is currently a student earning her Bachelor's Degree in English Writing at Millikin University. She works for the Decaturian, the school newspaper, as a writer and copy-editor. She hopes to write the Great American Novel someday, and, while that goal sounds as generic as Wonder Bread, it's still a great achievement for an aspiring author to have. Right?

Rebekah M. Icenesse

is set to graduate in May 2020 with a Bachelor's Degree in English Writing from Millikin University. She has an emphasis in Creative Writing and is a double minor in French and Publishing & Editing. She has worked as a journalist and editor for *The Decaturian* and *BURST* Magazine. She has been writing stories since she was little and aspires to become a novelist. Her writings show off her voice that she does not always verbally use. Even when she's silent, her mind is always speaking and creating ideas of the next thing to write.

Alex V. Miller

is a Professor at Millikin University where he teaches all levels of acting and stage combat. He also serves as Coordinator of Performance, Mainstage Director, Resident Fight Director, and is founder of and Executive Director for

Shakespeare Corrected. His professional performance career has taken him from coast to coast, though he currently lives on a small farm in Hammond, IL with his wife and two children.

Authors

Anonymous
participates in Shakespeare Corrected at the DCC.

Megan Batty
was born in Fort Bragg, North Carolina in 1997 while her father was stationed there. She moved to Stonington, Illinois when she was four years old. She will graduate from Millikin University in 2019 with a Bachelor of Arts in English Writing and a minor in Environmental Studies. She is a member of Delta Delta Delta, Delta Epsilon chapter, the Millikin University Sapphires Dance Team, and Burlesque Underground. She has been dancing for fourteen years and is very passionate about it. It is her favorite thing to do, and she says it is what defines her.

Dwight G. Brown, Jr.
is an African American male raised by a single mother of five. Dwight is no stranger to hardships, racial discrimination and police among them. He previously published an essay on police brutality in the very first volume of Brill's Critical Storytelling series, *Critical Storytelling in Millennial Times*. Despite all the negativity he has faced in life, Dwight has overcome each obstacle thrown his way. Dwight obtained his undergrad in Communications at Millikin University, where he went on to obtain his MBA. He is the father of a beautiful little girl, with a little boy on the way. Dwight now resides in Dallas, Texas, and manages at the Downtown TGI Fridays.

Sandra Brown
is and a long-time participant of the DCC's Shakespeare Corrected and a doctoral student in California Coast University's Ed.D. program. She has her BA from Ohio University and Masters from California State University, both of which she earned while incarcerated. Brown was a 28-year-old college student and mother living in Chicago when sentenced to more than two decades behind bars. She writes to work out frustrations and anger and to channel them into something positive: change. She says: "I'm living proof that life doesn't have to be over. This doesn't have to be the end. This could actually be the beginning of something greater." When released, she hopes to teach in the Department of Corrections.

Soren Belle

is not her real name. She is a butch lesbian with far too many emotions and far too few patient baristas willing to listen to her cry into a macchiato.

Kathryn Coffey

has been wanting to write and share her own stories since pre-school. Literally, since pre-school. She is currently a student earning her Bachelor's Degree in English Writing at Millikin University. She works for the Decaturian, the school newspaper, as a writer and copy-editor. She hopes to write the Great American Novel someday, and while that goal sounds as generic as Wonder Bread, it's still a great achievement for an aspiring author to have. Right?

Kelly Cunningham

was born and raised in small town Cary, Illinois. She is a storyteller on the stage and is transitioning in her piece to a storyteller on paper. She graduated in 2019 with a Bachelor of Fine Arts in Musical Theater.

Paiten Hamilton

is a self-published author, who received her Bachelor's degree in English from Millikin in 2018. Hamilton is furthering her education at New York Film Academy in Los Angeles. In her free time, Hamilton loves to make and edit her own Youtube videos.

Kathlyn J. Housh

graduated from Millikin University in 2018 with a degree in Sociology. A strong advocate for restorative justice, she is involved as a community partner in the local Teen Justice Program. In addition, she is a member of the Phi Kappa Phi Honor Society, Alpha Sigma Lambda Honor Society, and Sociology Club. She has been honored with making the Dean's List on more than one occasion during her academic career. Not only is Kathlyn a strong advocate for restorative justice, she is a firm believer in transforming the lives with which she comes in contact. Her passion for helping individuals realize who they are is apparent in her essay *Living a Life with Invisible Bars*.

Rebekah M. Icenesse

graduated in May 2020 and is currently obtaining a Bachelor's Degree in English Writing at Millikin University. She has an emphasis in Creative Writing and is a double minor in French and Publishing & Editing. She has worked as a journalist and editor for *The Decaturian* and BURST Magazine. She has been writing stories since she was little and aspires to become a novelist. Her writings show off her voice that she does not always verbally use. Even when she's silent, her mind is always speaking and creating ideas of the next thing to write about.

Kala Keller

is a recent graduate of Millikin University. She has over ten years of experience in creative thinking with a B.F.A. in Acting and extensive experience in insightful journalism, poetry, and haiku. You can see some of her other work in Randy Brooks' *The Art of Reading and Writing Haiku: A Reader Response Approach.* Kala resides in the greater Chicagoland area with her partner Logan and their two loving, free-roam rabbits. She plans to get a Master's degree in the fine arts field, and she hopes to travel the world.

Jelisa Lovette

received her GED and participated in Shakespeare Corrected while incarcerated at the DCC. She is a gifted poet who uses writing as a way to cope and to explore her thoughts inside and outside the prison walls. Through her poems, she expresses her desires to be free from the spiritual cage she is in and searches for her own purpose in life after release.

Bric Martin

is a rising fiction writer, who often dabbles in other forms. He's an editor for Bronze Man books and the winner of the Millikin University 2017 Novella Writing competition. Someday, he hopes to be resting on your bookshelf, or among a stack of magazines on the floor of your lavatory.

Amanda Minetti

was raised in northern Illinois in a small town known as Manhattan. She grew up with a music and theatre background, but because of her passion for animals she graduated with a degree in Biology at Millikin University. She will graduate in 2019 and be "living the dream" as they say.

Laura Nearing

was born in Wood Dale, Illinois and graduated from Millikin University in Spring 2019. While at Millikin, she was a Institute for Science and Entrepreneurship fellow. She is studying veterinary science at the University of Illinois, Urbana, works at Northgate Pet Clinic in Decatur, IL, and volunteers for the Decatur & Macon County Animal Shelter Foundation.

Angie Oakes

passed her GED exam while incarcerated. She was transferred to and from several different prisons across the state before completing her sentence at the Decatur Correctional Center. She's written prose and poetry for this volume. Through her writing, she works to better understand herself and improve her life before being released.

Claire Prendergast

was born in Joliet, Illinois in 1990. A major comic book and anime nerd, Prendergast has had a passion for art and storytelling her entire life. She graduated from Millikin University in May of 2018 with a BFA in Studio Art and a Psychology minor. She believes that art-making of any kind is inherently therapeutic and can help us become more actualized persons. She previously published an essay on the opioid crisis in the very first volume of Brill's Critical Storytelling series, *Critical Storytelling in Millennial Times*.

Cara Quiett

participated in Shakespeare Corrected and Dr. Braniger's writing workshop the last two years before her release from the DCC. She says of her time in prison: "Being sequestered in a prison enlightened me. Having every choice taken away, I realized that the only things that I could control were my thoughts and emotions. It was freeing! I lost so many years to prison but it was the price I had to pay. To free myself, from myself."

J. M. Spence

is a senior at Millikin University, working towards a Bachelor of Science in psychology, and preparing for a PhD in behavioral neuroscience.

Noah Villarreal

was born and raised in Austin, Texas. He has spent most of his life in the theatre, performing in shows all across the Austin community. He found his way to Millikin University for a Bachelor in Fine Arts in Musical Theatre which he received in Spring 2019.

Alisha Walker

participates in Shakespeare Corrected and performed her collaborative poetry piece at the Spring 2018 DCC Poetry Slam.

Prologue

Alex V. Miller

I was raised in rural Kansas, which was a perfect breeding ground, not just for livestock, but for imagination. As a child of 11, I was a rather radical fan of comic books. I had multiple subscriptions and waited anxiously every month for their arrival so I could religiously read the trials and tribulations of my idols.

Walking home from the bus stop, a good half mile (uphill, both ways), I would be Wolverine, Cyclops, or my favorite character—myself. I created in my mind an avatar with a variance of powers including flight. That was what I desired. More than anything, I craved the ability to fly. The aspiration was never to look down on people, but was to see the world from a new perspective. A vantage point and experience that would grant me an elusive freedom from the limitations I faced as a "mere mortal."

In our backyard, there was a dog pen with five stalls and a tin roof just rusty enough to give one tetanus. Next to the dog pen was a large stack of concrete blocks just wobbly enough to collapse and kill oneself. After school, day after day I would climb the blocks and steady myself on the edge of the tin roof. I would look at the ground, at my limitations, and sweat. I would look at the pristine blue sky, my potential, and pray. "Please God, let me fly." I would leap, hang in the humid air for a second under my own limited power, and inevitably, fall.

The plan was to believe. If I believed enough, I would be able to fly. If I trusted enough, I could be more than what I was. If my faith was strong enough, I could alter my world and be freed from the concerns of the everyday. I would be able to escape the trauma that shaped my life and atone for the mistakes I had made. However, years passed, and my dream of flight was circumvented. I stopped leaping from rooftops and began leaping into the everyday. I followed impulses and took educated risks to better my life. Which brings me to this moment.

In reading the pages of this book, I am reminded of how fortunate I am. I find myself humbled by the selflessness of those who have freely given of their time and talents. More than anything, I am grateful that the dream of an 11-year-old boy has been made possible. For in the love of a family, the generosity of colleagues, and the help of countless friends, I find myself lifted by others into the sincere miracle of flight.

© KONINKLIJKE BRILL NV, LEIDEN, 2020 | DOI: 10.1163/9789004441651_001

CHAPTER 1

A Prisoner's Melody

Sandra Brown, Jelisa Lovette and Alisha Walker

Sandra Brown:

Buried alive
But I will survive these
Twenty-two in D.O.C.
Charged with murder
In the first degree.
'Cause I didn't wanna d-i-e
Buried alive.
I gotta survive these
Twenty-two in D.O.C.
Charged with murder
In the first degree.
'Cause I didn't wanna d-i-e...

I don't know if doing state time
At one-hundred-percent
Has set in yet.
I guess that depends on what 'set' means.

Fear set in with a gun cocked in my face.
Flight set in when fatal fight took place.
Grief set in when Momma said she died.
Loss set in when family on me lied.

Remorse, regret, and real raw pain set in.
Tears, truth, and strength brought healing from within.

Time, much too precious.
Once it's gone, it's gone.
And I can never have THAT moment—
The best of THAT moment—

© KONINKLIJKE BRILL NV, LEIDEN, 2020 | DOI: 10.1163/9789004441651_002

The most of THAT moment again.
When did this time set in?

Contemplation ticks.
And retrospection tocs.
And devastation picks.
And hopelessness it knocks.
So faith stays fixed
And endurance locked
Out that unwelcome vagabond
Attempting to abscond with my—
With my i-den-ti-ty

I serve this life, but state time won't set in.
The day it does, it means I let in.
I would not serve the kind of time that binds.
I serve the time that best serves humankind.

Jelisa Lovette:

Yeah, son. I'm serving nine right along wit you.
Different ways different days
But still serving life is what it all boils down to.
I had it good coming up, how?
Look what I'm forced to go through now.
Da food I'm forced to eat, da things I get forced to do now.
Da cloths I'm forced to wear, white grey, maroon, blue,
Blue—it matched my mood sometimes.
Bad ways remind me of my hood days.
Hustling wit' nothing but money on my mind.
Right now wishin' I could get dat call from Steve,
Just to tell me he only got forty-nine.
I'd take it without even think' twice, just being honest.
I was serving a lot more than life.

Sex-hugs-drugs-love-da plug?
I didn't think about, nor care who I was hurtin'.
None of it really hit me till da day da judge was reading me my verdict.
But even then I was numb to da simple fact dat I was facing real time.

No longer able to grind, settin' like da sun, gotta wait twelve hours.
But fo me, twelve years cut in half before I can pop back out to shine.
Damn man what the fuck was I really out there thinking?
Pops died and I just lost my damn mind.
Now I'm stuck serving time,
because I wouldn't drop da dime.
Damn.

Alisha Walker:

Damn Roc, that shit real.
Plenty of nights feeling claustrophobic.
Staring up at the molded ceiling in the cook county cell.
For real.
My whole life has been confined.
Childhood locked inside.
Taking care of a baby that wasn't mine.
Loving a control freak.
Searching for my Dad.
Now caged behind locked doors.
Yeah, freedom is something I've never
imagined could be real.
Damn near killed myself twice.
But that shit ain't in my blood.
I survive, raised to fight.
I guess we're all rueing life
In some shape or form.
Sentenced to 16 at 50%.
They gave me the hope that
I could go home while I'm still
Young, yet
Just because I'm eligible
don't make it available,

Belittling myself being something
That I'm not.
This shit aint the cook for the streets
Out there you do what you gotta do to eat.
When did I lose that hunger?
Getting homesick every time it's summer.

Constantly being told no,
I focus so hard on leaving this hell hole.
One thing I've learned is how much I want to live free,
Do everything I've dreamed of,
So you see
I'm a better person and all that.
I'll be damned if I come back.
I've corrected as much as I'm gonna
Correct in the department of corrections.
I'm done trying to conform,
I'm my own creation reborn,
I can't serve life anymore.

CHAPTER 2

Barcode

Sandra Brown

One of the harshest side effects of doing time is confusing where you are with who you are. The systemic identicide that you undergo is traumatic at best; it starts with that very first ID picture that you are forced to take. Those who've been there know; it's the one that shows your hair uncombed, your face seemingly stoic but in reality, numb with shock and confusion, and your eyes redder than the ripest strawberries in the middle of your last summer as a free woman. I took that picture eighteen years ago; only the back of my head was completely bald then. You look at the picture and can't begin to figure out who it is, but that's the purpose. Then alongside this unrecognizable creaturesque human reads a barcode, a series of numbers, and two names: the one you gave the law, and the one the law gives you.

"Inmate or "Offender" is now part of your name.

I was branded with two even, memorable numbers: 20000005402 for fourteen months; after that, R35900. From time to time, I look at that number and try to comprehend its significance. What does the "R" represent? Is it only for female prisoners? Was I the 35,900th prisoner to enter IDOC (Illinois Department of Corrections) that year? I muse over the barcode and can't help but wonder how long I'd been locked up before I came to prison. Two rapes and a string of abusive relationships kept me locked up, being a high school dropout for a while kept me locked out, and twelve years of alcoholism kept me locked down. What's frighteningly disturbing to me is that I had no understanding of this until well after I took that first ID picture. Indeed, prison is not the only place that holds inmates.

Whether I ponder such things in futility remains questionable, yet I am compelled to do so. My real name, Sandra, is Greek. It is short for Alexandra, and it means "Helper/Defender of Mankind." How ironic is it that I am sentenced to 8,030 days in IDOC for defending myself? But that's another topic for another time. The pictures get better or worse over the years, depending on the kindness of time. But who the law says you are remains the largest, most prominent thing printed across the top of your ID-INMATE. At the very bottom, where insignificant information is listed, reads my real name; and somewhere in the middle sits this huge barcode and a series of numbers. What does this mean? Does not the over worn, underpatched, ill-fitting

© KONINKLIJKE BRILL NV, LEIDEN, 2020 | DOI: 10.1163/9789004441651_003

navy-blue pants that never reach my ankles and once white-now-beige state issue smock clarify enough my station in this place? If not, then initiation and the culture shock behind it will more than show you who the law says you are. Albuquerque

I remember being herded into the first of what would be four prisons. Reception and classification (A.K.A. the "X" House) is where you get branded with your second number, strip searched, and cavity checked. Every piercing, tattoo, or scar gets inventoried on a sheet of paper and entered on a website database for all to see. Finally, you are forced to live in cramped quarters; complete with steel toilets attached to sinks from which you fear getting sick if you use because every conceivable germ and bodily secretion looks like it still resides there. Yes, you share this assigned space with another prisoner, but that's not the only company you keep. Cockroaches, spiders, water bugs big enough to fight mice, and muscular rats invade your things, your bed, and when they're hungry, your body and your property box. The only view (if you are fortunate enough to get one) is of fences, barbed wire, adjacent brick walls with slitted, dirt-gray windows and cow fields.

For seven weeks, I oiled what was left of my hair with pats of margarine from the chow hall. When I had no more soap, I showered every other day as allowed in mold infested, rusty showers that reeked of urine and lacked hot water, using shampoo. By week five, I remember standing at the door of my cell for nearly six hours on second shift, begging an officer for soap. He was a round, coffee-complexioned black man with condescending eyes who stood no taller than my nose. I waited every time he asked me to give him a minute. I waited in between his wing checks to remind him that I was still there, waiting. I waited at his desk after returning from chow, but he ordered me back to my cell and told me I'd get it when I'd get it. I waited at the door, peering through the narrow, cage-like chuckhole as he stood for over thirty minutes flirting with my then next-door cellie.

By 9pm, I knew he'd never come back after count, so I made the mistake of interrupting him. He stormed off, and the relief I felt of finally getting that bar of soap was quickly replaced by the humiliation of him throwing it at me and slamming the door. He called me a worsen bitch, as if I were some debilitating condition and not a person, and he told me not to ask him for shit else before resuming his conversation with my next-door cellie. I remember pressing my face against the slitted window to hide it from my bunkie, whom I'd heard giggling, I knew that the tears falling from my face were hot, angry, and sad, but I fought not to feel it in my heart. What I couldn't escape, however, was the fact that I was being broken down, stripped of who I am. The view screamed this at me. The dirty, dilapidated shack in the middle of the cornfield matched that very first ID picture I took.

That would be the first of countless attempts at identicide against me. The process by which it demeans or dehumanizes can make you confuse where you are with who you are if you are not determined, resilient, and careful.

CHAPTER 3

Caged

Jelisa Lovette

Silence
Drowned out all the sounds,
Of metal scrapping
Against walls, and floors, wars,
Unsettled scores, swollen hands
Blistering, beating on doors, sweat,
Bleeding thru pores. Steaming,
Screaming profanities, such calamities
I've suffered by my own doing
I've suffered, unable to buffer
The blows of my own fist
Unable to muffle the sounds
Of those voices dat remind
Me of the choices I made.
I make it wit my own hands
I braid the rope from which
I hang myself, in a noose.
As I dangle from this tree,
Barely living, barely
Free, barely me.
I am cut me loose.
Please I can't
Breathe, I can't see,
I'm lost somewhere in between
My dreams and nightmares
And one excuse
Reality introduced,
Insanity included barely alive.
Unable to cope with the pain
Of my thoughts
So I don't think,

© KONINKLIJKE BRILL NV, LEIDEN, 2020 | DOI: 10.1163/9789004441651_004

Nor do I remember
Memory lane
Is a dead-end street filled wit pain.

CHAPTER 4

The Forbidden & the Prohibited

Soren Belle

I

Mankind has manufactured many evils, but perhaps one of our most insidious and destructive creations are borders. Our society is bursting with ingrained dichotomies. Nationality, race, gender, sexuality are considered obvious and unchangeable. In truth, the only certain thing about such binaries is that they are never as clear cut as those dividing imagine them to be.

A strikingly relevant text in the landscape of today's America is Gloria Anzaldua's landmark work: *Borderlands/La Frontera: The New Mestiza*. Her thesis is a blend of prose and poetry, English, Spanish, and unique dialects that are comprehensible only to native bilinguals. Anzaldua's literary canon and work in academia marks her as a pioneer in feminist, queer, and Chicana cultural theory.

Gloria grew up on the border between Texas and Mexico. She called the jagged edge a "1,950 mile-long-open-wound/dividing a pueblo, a culture. This is my home, this thin edge of barbed wire" (Anzaldua, 1999, p. 3).

I do not live on the war-torn crests of an imperial power and its ravaged neighbor. I cannot know the burden of living in a land so divided, skin tone and heritage determining the entirety of your life before you get a chance to live it.

But when Gloria writes of those who live in the land between borders, I marvel at how she manages to describe something that sounds so much like my home.

The other day my classmates were joking about how they weren't sure how many of their cousins were also their uncles or aunts. They come from small communities and families connected by marriage, making such affairs complicated. With a chuckle, I mentioned, "When I was a kid and I first learned about slavery, I flipped out. I went home and demanded to know whether any of my mom's family had owned my dad's family."

I still remember that conversation with my parents as they explained. My mother's forefathers were Scandinavian immigrants from the early twentieth century. My father's ancestors were, as far as we can tell, from sugar plantations in Jamaica, and were free by the turn of the nineteenth century.

© KONINKLIJKE BRILL NV, LEIDEN, 2020 | DOI: 10.1163/9789004441651_005

That knowledge soothed me.

It helped me feel like less of a contradiction.

II

Writer James Baldwin was once asked by a reporter: "When you were starting out as a writer you were black, impoverished, homosexual. You must have said to yourself, "Gee, how disadvantaged can I get?"

He reportedly replied with a simple, "No. I felt I'd hit the jackpot. It was so outrageous, you had to find a way to use it."

James used his oh-so-outrageous life to speak out for his people, in the multitude of communities in which they existed. For the poor, for the black, for the gay.

For three years he worked as a Youth Minister, as many misguided young homosexuals do. He described that service as, "the most frightening time of my life, and quite the most dishonest, and the resulting hysteria lent great passion to my sermons—for a while."

There is a curious fever that possesses preachers who try to teach doctrine they do not believe. Thankfully, the human soul's capacity for cognitive dissonance is impressive. It can take those doubts, the stress of internal contradiction and transmute it into rabid devotion. Liberated from the realm of reasonability, one can stand firm on a false foundation.

Some call such hypocrisy immoral, dishonest. But for lesbian, gay, bisexual, trans, and queer people, existence itself is a contradiction. From the early days of childhood onwards, the experiences and emotions of the queer person is at odds with the society in which they exist. Friction, when makeup is roughly scrubbed off a little boy's face. Friction, when a dress's lace collar scratches at her neck. Friction, little fingers flipping the thin golden pages of Grandma's bible. Knees aching from hours spent at their bedside, begging for answers. Eyes burning from searching a reflection for any hint of truth.

Friction, friction, friction—and then flame.

That's how some of us survive being too many things at once. White knuckles on the side of the pulpit, reminding the congregation that everyone faces tempting thoughts. Strength, of course, is the resistance of temptation. The repression of desire.

That's how some of us survive. We burst into flame. It's dangerous, unsustainable. The fallout is wicked. The ashes of faith are a cold place.

At the end of his holy career, Baldwin stood alone, alienated from congregation, community, and country.

III

Gloria calls the indeterminate spaces between two worlds a borderland. A borderland, she says, "is a vague and undetermined place created by the emotional residue of an unnatural boundary. The prohibited and forbidden are its inhabitants" (Anzaldua, 1999, p. 25). The artificiality and assumed inevitability of borders is a key theme of her writings, and her critiques are well-substantiated.

Texas had been a state for, as of Gloria's birth, under a century. Its age is nothing to the mountains at its northwest corner, the vast Gulf of Mexico to the southeast. Texas is a concept in its infancy. On either side of the border lies people with ancestors from pre-colonization Americas, from Europe, from Africa and Asia and all over the world- yet one side holds Texans and the other, foreigners.

In a time of bathroom bills and trans rights, science is uncovering more and more evidence that intersex people have always existed. Women are sometimes born with Y chromosomes, men sometimes have ovaries. In American culture, we only recently have developed the vocabulary to comprehend people whose bodies or souls fall outside of the binaries of sex and gender. Yet sociologists can prove that the gender binary is a quirk of the modern, Westernized world, rather than a stanchion of humanity.

Dichotomies are the creation of man. Nature creates spectrums. When these spectrums are construed, people get left out, left behind.

Thus: the inhabitants of the borderlands. As Gloria calls them, "the prohibited and the forbidden" (Anzaldua, 1999, p. 3).

IV

In 1949, tucked away in the beauty of Paris, James Baldwin fell in love. He was a black man that left behind a nation that deemed him second-class, a culture that considered him sinful and deviant. Yet here, in the streets of Paris, he met Lucien Happersberger. The photographs of them are striking, Baldwin dark and Lucien pale against him. For a while, they took the borders they were given and traversed them- country lines meant nothing, race meant nothing, gender and the love for it was irrelevant. They were beloved, and that was beautiful.

The forbidden and the prohibited lived in peace with the world that rejected them. The multiplicity of identity was no longer frictional within Baldwin, but rather blended, in harmony.

V

Gloria referred to her sexual and gender identity in many terms, but her most prevalent identity was 'lesbian.' Her existence as such, she posited, was a transgression against many aspects of her society, from the variations in the human form, to the assumption of gender roles, to the definitions of sex and love. In *Borderlands*, she writes:

> There is something compelling about being both male and female, about having an entry into both worlds. Contrary to some psychiatric tenets, half and halfs are not suffering from a confusion of sexual identity, or even from a confusion of gender. What we are suffering from is an absolute despot duality that says we are able to be only one or the other... But I, like other queer people, am two in one body, both male and female. I am the embodiment of the heiros gamos: the coming together of opposite qualities within. (Anzaldúa, 1999, p. 41)

In the narrative of the oppressor, those who fail to perfectly inhabit one world over another fail to belong anywhere. The truth is far, far more beautiful than that. We inherit a cracked world from the dividers who came before us, but we are not doomed to live broken lives. The forbidden and the prohibited may be outcasts, but the borderlands are a place of creation.

The forbidden are more than neither, the prohibited are more than both. They are something new, something beyond the comprehension of the constructs they are commanded to conform to. They do not exist between the boundaries as much as they do beyond the limitations of borders.

VI

There came a week where I was to receive an award at a university assembly, and present an academic paper the next day. When my parents received the invitation, my father said he wanted to come down.

That semester I had returned from winter break and paid a friend $5 to shave my head. I began to throw away old, ratty, lacy clothes I had worn for years, and began wearing crisp men's polos, button down shirts. Pictures on facebook of me proudly sporting a tie, blazer slung over my shoulder, reportedly did not go over well at home.

I texted my dad, and I tried to be civil. "I've been dressing differently lately. I don't wear dresses anymore, or much jewelry. I wanted to let you know that if you come down to see me, I'll be wearing a white shirt and tie."

I even added some emotion, hoping the honesty would help open some doors. "I'm worried that when you see me like that, you will feel like you wasted the trip."

I didn't tell him about heiros gamos, about existing in worlds both male and female. I didn't tell him about the first night I came out to myself, all the nights after, where I declared the truth to my reflection, facing myself again and again until the words didn't make me flinch anymore. I didn't tell him about the girls in the springtime and the summer and the fall, the dances and the coffee dates and the breakup. The twisting in my gut the first time I wore a tie, I asked her out, I shaved my head, I held her hand.

I didn't tell him about the families in Walmart that glare at me, the whispers when I try to buy work boots or a button down. I don't know how to show him that I was born in borderlands, I cannot help being a transgressor. That if I am made to live here, then I may as well explore and make it home.

I just said that I dress differently than I used to.

The conversation didn't go well. It ended with him informing me that he would no longer respond to my messages.

VII

In 1952, James Baldwin had his heart broken, when his Lucien married a wonderful young woman. The two men remained close for years. Baldwin died with Lucien at his side.

VIII

As a young person, it means the world to know that people who came before me were like me. As Baldwin himself once said, "You read something which you thought only happened to you, and you discover that it happened 100 years ago to Dostoyevsky. This is a very great liberation for the suffering, struggling person, who always thinks that he is alone" (Baldwin, 1989, p. 21).

I am grateful to Baldwin, to Anzaldua, to all of the writers and activists like them, who dared to be honest in a time when authenticity demanded courage. I am grateful that their stories serve as countless testaments to this; the people of the Borderlands; the forbidden and the prohibited are many, many things. But they are not alone.

We are not alone.

References

Anzaldúa, G. (1999). *Borderlands: La frontera.* Aunt Lute Books.

Baldwin, J. (1963). *The fire next time.* Dial Press.

Baldwin, J., Standley, F. L., & Pratt, L. H. (1989). *Conversations with James Baldwin.* University of Mississippi Press.

CHAPTER 5

Truth or Dare

Sandra Brown

Truth, dare, double-dare, promise, or repeat?
I dare tell on truth.
Eight-year-old elbow met pavement
learning to ride my bike.
That's my story...
That's a story...
No. That's a goddamn lie.
Truth burns memory
like a cigarette burns flesh.
Too young to smoke then,
too old to forget now.
You tell, you die—
late truth become lie.
They say the truth hurts...
but I wish that was all it did.

Truth, dare, double-dare, promise, or repeat?
Broken promises repeat
like scratched records,
loud mistakes,
and loose change
stuck in pissy couches.
Innocence smothered in stained stenches.
Screaming couches
tell things they know,
and things others don't.

Truth, dare, double-dare, promise, or repeat?
I dare exhume
the broken looking glass
who won't play make-believe
with me and Maybelline.
Looking back

© KONINKLIJKE BRILL NV, LEIDEN, 2020 | DOI: 10.1163/9789004441651_006

at the looking glass
looking back at me
I see
with my inside eyes
I see
with unpunchable eyes.

Beauty for cigarette ashes.
Unburned return
to innocence lost.

I dare unquiet the big little girl
unafraid to let you touch her story.
I dare unmask my Self,
and see countless faces like me.

CHAPTER 6

The People I Met When the Sky Went Dark

Bric Martin

7:07 A.M.

Seven minutes behind schedule due to a low velocity collision with a two-foot brick wall inconveniently positioned in our blind spot, my colleague and friend, Ward Gurgeh and I take off from Decatur, IL to Carbondale in his mom's now dented Impala to witness the 2017 total solar eclipse. We both travel in professional capacities, Ward scientific and I journalistic, but our relaxed demeanor and casual dress may mislead folks to confuse us with ordinary ogglers, or with Southern Illinois University students who've been granted the day off school as an opportunity to celebrate this rare astrological phenomenon. However, for Ward and I, this is no day of leisure. We are all business.

Ward is a degreed physicist, whose resume includes three papers on theoretical astrophysics; one of which served as a criticism of Stephen Hawking's theories regarding the density of dark matter, and received enough attention in the scientific community to earn him a firm handshake with famed astrophysicist, Neil deGrasse Tyson. Ward is, by definition, a genius. I may not hold such merits, but I strive to be (and refuse to fall short of) a *great* novelist. As of now, I am unpublished. While I wait for an acceptance letter from Penguin Random House, I approach writing with a fat head and a fake-it-till-you-make-it attitude. So here I am today, riding shotgun to the biggest brain in my contact list, transcribing fun facts about the sun as Ward spits them over his energy drink.

"The photons we're seeing today were created inside the sun 100,000 years ago," he says. "Neutrinos tell us what's happening in the sun currently, while photons tell us what was happening when they were created."

I nod my head like I understand, even though I'm doing more stenographing than active listening. Typically, I'd engage with this fun fact and contribute some facts of my own. Theoretical physics is not my field of expertise, but I know a thing or two about the cosmos. My grasp of astrophysics is halfway between a Facebook understanding and that of a true enthusiast. I could pass a 200 level astronomy course with flying colors. I like to tell people that I have an *artistic* understanding in multiple areas of science, which basically means that I've memorized enough fun facts to impress people at parties. I've read a few books, and have seen every episode of *Cosmos*, (both the Carl Sagan original

© KONINKLIJKE BRILL NV, LEIDEN, 2020 | DOI: 10.1163/9789004441651_007

and the reboot with Neil deGrasse Tyson) but I'm not exactly spending my Saturday nights calculating the density of dark matter with accounting for the Doppler effect. However, if you do catch me on a Saturday night, I'll be happy to give you the gist of what Ward has said regarding the matter. Essentially, Hawking may have flubbed the numbers a bit.

"Neutrinos hit the Earth at a rate of 100 billion per square centimeter per second," says Ward. "There's like, a fuck-ton passing through us right now."

I'm too busy stenographing and haven't had enough coffee to think of anything smart to say back to him. Because I'm not providing my usual commentary to his science lesson, he must feel as though I'm not listening.

"What do 100 billion neutrinos and I have in common?"

I've been close friends with Ward for over a year now. In that time, I've developed a sixth sense for recognizing his setups. Feeling guilty for not engaging with him before, I decide to take the bait, peering up from my notepad for the first time since we got in the car, and responding with a simple, yet curious "What?" Ward has an ornery, childish smirk.

"We've both been through Uranus."

I furrow my brow and try to restrain my laughter, not wanting to give him the satisfaction. Because I try to suppress it, my soft throat giggle involuntarily turns into a tight cheeked elephant call. Ward is chuckling so hard, he has a slight nose whistle. We're both night owls. Lack of sleep, in tandem with the joke's pure Wardliness has us both slap-happy. If anyone else had made this crack, I'd be repulsed, but Ward is the only guy I know who can successfully couple molecular physics with a high school locker room joke. Regaining my composure, I return to my notes as we merge onto the highway.

7:25 A.M.

Before leaving Decatur, we stop for fuel and breakfast pizza at a petrol station on the edge of town. We overhear other customers saying that they too are traveling south to catch a view of totality, rather than a lame view of the cloud shrouded partial eclipse that'll be visible here in Decatur. Our *Hunk of Pizza* is labeled *Caution: Delicious!* I take a nibble in the parking lot and consider filing a lawsuit against the Shell station for false advertising. As I wait for Ward to finish pumping, I take stock of our supplies one last time. Our inventory includes four cigarettes, three cans of LaCroix, a bag of gummy bears, popcorn, two notebooks, fifteen writing utensils, $32.05 we've pooled together for lunch and dinner, fruit flavored Tootsie rolls, a handful of instant coffee packets, four granola bars, an energy drink, a graphing calculator, a digital audio recorder, and two homemade pinhole projectors because neither one of us geniuses had the foresight to purchase eclipse glasses in advance.

8:45 A.M.

Traffic is hellacious. According to our GPS, the usual three hour drive to Carbondale is going to be extended to four and a half. We take an alternate route through rural communities such as Cowden and Hillsboro, expecting to shave at least half an hour off the GPS's interstate prediction. We're clearly not the only people to have this idea, as getting off the highway somehow adds an extra fifteen minutes to our drive. As an area local, I know that these towns are usually empty and uneventful. Very seldom are they burdened with traffic jams. Local residents in their immaculate green yards seem both bewildered and annoyed by all the commotion. Flabbergasted may be the best term. Not only are there hundreds, perhaps thousands of cars, but half of the drivers act as though they've never been in a town without stoplights. Currently, the succession of vehicles between us and the next stop sign goes: truck, Prius, truck, Mini Cooper, truck, Corolla, truck, truck.

People move to towns like Cowden to get away from hubbub and honking cars. But on this seemingly ordinary Monday, the fuss of the city has arrived at their doorstep, blocking their driveway and littering on their Kentucky bluegrass. A man on a crotch rocket passes every stopped car, and runs the stop sign driving about 50 m.p.h. I bite the head off a gummy bear to make it resemble some of the drivers.

9:32 A.M.

If I were superstitious, I'd say that karma is coming to punish me for the earlier comment I made about the Decatur sky, and all the other spectators may suffer as collateral damage. The cloud cover gets worse the nearer we drive to Carbondale. I check the weather app on my phone to confirm what my naked eye can already see: a blanket of stratocumulus clouds covers most of the sky and is likely to remain for the next several hours. They're patchy and fast moving, this could either play to our favor or to our disadvantage. If there are clouds obscuring our view just before the eclipse, they might drift past in time for totality. If the sun is in an opening, a cloud could float in our way just as totality is about to occur.

Of course, several other possibilities are probable and there is no need to hypothesize a false dichotomy. However, the point still remains. The traffic jams, our gas money, my research and stenographing, and the plight of every curious traveler could all be for nothing. This whole trip is a roll of the dice.

10:14 A.M.

Ward needs to find a bathroom and I recommend that he goes in an empty LaCroix can. He says there's no way he'll fit through the sharp hole, so I drop a fun fact, letting him know that fully grown octopi can fit their entire body through a standard keyhole. In the village of Sesser, we stop at a gas station called Huck's. Due to the sign that depicts a hillbilly boy chewing on a blade of wheat grass, in tandem with the fact that we're leaving the land of Lincoln and entering Twain territory, I assume the store's name is a reference to *The Adventures of Huckleberry Finn.* Pointing that out, Ward responds to me in a no-duh tone.

There's nowhere to park, so Ward gets out while I stay with the car.

He walks to the gas station, but turns at the door as the line to the bathroom begins on the welcome mat. I ask him again if he'd like to pee in an empty LaCroix can. He tells me to drive to the next station. It ends up being just as packed, so he decides to do his business in a soy field while I keep lookout.

On our way out of town, a Baptist church sign reads, "DEAR LORD, IS CHRIST READY TO RETURN? GIVE US A SIGN, BLOT OUT THE SUN." Ward remarks that a solar eclipse should hardly be considered a sign of anything. Solar eclipses happen between two and four times a year at various locations around the globe. We don't notice every time it happens, because totality can only be viewed from a fifty-mile radius of an eclipse's nadir. Also, the position of an eclipse can be calculated and accurately predicted far before its occurrence.

Whoever posted this message knows in advance that the alleged sign (the eclipse) is going to be visible from their location. They prescribed a false meaning to a naturally occurring phenomenon to make it fit their religious agenda. It's a similar blind ascription to phenomena that lead the Inca to react to the eclipse by committing human sacrifice, and that led the ancient Vikings to think that a giant space-wolf was trying to eat the sun. Whether the sign maker's intentions are misguided, or blatantly selective, they should reevaluate their biases. I bite the head off another gummy bear.

11:34 A.M.

We finally arrive in Carbondale and the city is bumping. Ward and I haven't seen much yet, as we first detour to my friend Wendy's apartment. Wendy is a student at the local college, Southern Illinois University (SIU, home of the Sulkis!) and upon welcoming us, she makes a joke about being our tour guide for the day. Having never met Ward before, she has no idea which know-it-all physicist is about to hijack this tour. Wendy is highly intelligent, but her talents lay in media and music. If my scientific knowledge is riding shotgun, she'll be lucky to find a spot in the back seat.

We plop on the couch and watch the local weather channel until her friends, Emma and Griffin arrive. The meteorologist forecasts that the partial cloud cover will remain present for the rest of the day. Ward claims that the chances of the eclipse being visible are about 50/50, but I assume that's more of a guesstimation than a calculated measurement. Although I'm worked-up, Ward is used to being fog-blocked from phenomena. Over the years he's learned to cope.

I inform Wendy that we'd like to take part in some eclipse themed festivities before totality. In saying so, I unwittingly put her and her friends on a mission to smoke their bag of marijuana as fast as possible. Being that I'm there in an official journalistic capacity, and Ward in a scientific capacity, we decline the pot, although we're three times promised that it's "premium ganja." Once they're all stony baloney, we head to the streets.

SIU is infamous for excessive partying. Last Halloween (Carbondale's favorite day of debauchery), a few students celebrated by flipping a local police car outside a downtown bar while the fuzz were off dealing with some other delinquents. Today the atmosphere is similar. College students chug canned beer on the balconies of their apartments. Most of the males, including our new friend, Griffin, are wearing either aviator or wayfarer sunglasses and tank tops with marketable sayings on them, that either use *guns* as a double entendre for firearms and muscles, such as *SUN'S OUT GUNS OUT* and *WELCOME TO THE GUN SHOW*, or obsess over the word *bro*, (i.e. *COME AT ME BRO* and *BRO-BIDEN*).

It's still technically morning, but the bars circulate with half-drunken students. The bars at SIU are the kind of establishments that serve bacon, eggs, and beer on Sunday mornings. The kind of pubs that turn a light on above the bathroom to alert both bartenders and underage drinkers when there's a potential police presence. The kind of dives that have designated puke corners on the street side of their biergartens. From what Wendy tells me, these places are slightly more busy than on an ordinary Monday, but only slightly. For a moment, I'm disappointed that this is how students choose to celebrate such a beautiful event, but then I remember that the eclipse used to be celebrated with human sacrifice, so maybe getting hammered is a healthier alternative. I cannot judge.

Once every six months or so, when I'm reunited with my lifelong best friend who joined the Air Force after high school, we inevitably celebrate by getting unnecessarily wasted. Our lives have gone so far adjacent from one another that when we intersect, although we both crave genuine connection, the only way to achieve a sense of homeostasis is to drink until our livers betray us. I mean, we *really* put it down. Every time one of us is about to slow up, we peer pressure the other into taking another shot until we're both drunk enough to confess how deeply we miss each other. I suppose that some emotions, even the beautiful ones, are easier to confront after a few, or a few too many drinks. This reflection doesn't make me less disappointed in the other students. In turn, I'm also disappointed in myself.

11:46 A.M.

Griffin is not my usual company, but he seems like a sincere guy. His sincerity is exemplified in reaction to my inside jokes with Ward and our snarkiness. Ward points out that shadows are altered during a solar eclipse. Hearing this, mind-blown Griffin asks about Ward's professional and academic background. I speak for Ward, as he prefers not to brag for himself. After I provide a brief resume (references included), Griffin replies with a verbal "woah," then stares at the sidewalk for a while. Before we can ask about his major and career aspirations, Emma sees me writing in my notebook and asks what I'm frantically scratching. I tell her that I'm maybe potentially writing a story about the eclipse, and she *jumps jumps jumps,* clapping to punctuate each bounce. She tells me that while riding her bike this morning, she kept track of every state she saw on a license plate, then she recites the list without my asking.

"I saw twenty-seven states," she declares with a cheerleader's dagger. "Missouri, Kansas, Indiana, Georgia, Wisconsin, Maryland, South Carolina, Maine, Michigan, New York, Alabama, Virginia, Florida, Ohio, Kentucky, Colorado, Minnesota, Texas, Iowa, California, Tennessee, Maryland... Wait, did I already say Maryland? Make that twenty-six. New Jersey, North Carolina, Arkansas, Nevada, and New Mexico."

I'm impressed by her attention to detail, coupled with her complete lack of awareness when in regards to her surroundings. She claims to have spent two hours checking every license plate she passed, yet she tells me this while walking backwards and staring at her phone. People as graceful as her don't always need to look where they're going. I can't help but to imagine her morning bike ride as a Mr. Magoo style travesty, causing low velocity traffic accidents and slapstick chaos while she records license plates with one hand and texts in the other. Not to stereotype, but Emma seems like the kind of girl who does a lot of texting. The kind who buys designer handbags and hangs on the arm of guys in bro tanks. She was probably prom queen in high school, or at least had enough popularity to be a running member of the homecoming court. What makes her different from the prom queen cliché is that she did not peak in high school, nor will she in college. She escaped her small town and made it out into the world of apartment complex pool parties and fraternity house keg stands.

Now that she's had a taste of the good life, the party won't end here. Soon she'll be over the bro tank boys and she'll crave a different animal. She'll put her degree to use and get a safe job where she'll work for a decade before obtaining a six-figure title. She'll find a husband, a strong physical specimen who wears collared shirts and platinum watches: *bro tank 2.0*. They'll have two or three kids with biblical names that are uniform in both syllable count and alliteration, such as Jacob, Jerod, and Judith, or Adam, Ava, and Aaron. She'll buy a speed boat and a one-story house in the suburbs. A couple years later, she'll keep up with the Joneses by upgrading that speed boat to a house boat and selling her two-story townhouse for a three-story colonial house in a gated community around the block, where every house is a slightly modified version of its neighbor.

There, keeping up with the Joneses will be a different game. Rather than competing for the largest house, the unspoken competition will regard the greenest lawn and the most decorated children. Adam, Ava, and Aaron will likely be raised by a nanny, while Emma and Daddy focus their energies on buying more things they can't afford with their watch colored credit cards, until her life has become a completely different kind of cliché, and her youngest child accidentally refers to their hypothetical nanny as *Mommy*. Then she'll find a haphazard reason to impulsively fire the nanny, and for the first time since breastfeeding, she'll be stuck trying to figure out how to raise her three little angels, until she finally gives up on her picturesque life, fakes her own death, and starts a new family in a farm town like Cowden to get back to her roots... Either that, or soon she'll get over the party scene and use her degree to find a career that fulfills her both financially and spiritually. Maybe she'll have kids, maybe she won't.

Maybe I'll burn out as another wanna-be writer cliché, philosophizing from a cobblestone grain bin that I claim as a high tower, writing cliché stories in judgment of genuine people, with a pen in one hand and a torch in the other, imaging myself to be a mind beyond my time, restrained by the Facebook minds of contemporary people. And Griffin will live on to do whatever Griffin does. I still haven't inquired about that. And Ward will be Ward, making blue jokes and quantifying the currently unquantified. And speculation will continue to reflect more about the speculator than it does about the speculated. And the world will go round and round, occasionally aligning with the sun and the moon to black out the sky, without concern for our equations, our sacrifices and prayers, our writers and homecoming queens, our Cowdens and Carbondales, or the status and titles we use to stereotype each other into cliché little boxes.

12:05 P.M.

Carnies have commandeered a community parking lot to hawk cheaply made tee shirts for the price of a confederate flag decal, which they also happen to be selling in a booth across the street. Other wares include truck nuts, pocket knives, license plate frames, homemade ice cream, trucker hats, lemon shake-ups, funnel cake, and just about anything else you'd expect to find at a county fair. Aside from fatty food and cheap novelty items, Ward and I are lucky enough to find actual eclipse glasses for only $6.00 a pair! His are jet black and make him look like Cyclops from the *X-Men* comic books. Mine are American Flag patterned and would be more stylish if I were wearing a bro-tank. We try to use our new glasses to see the partial eclipse, but the cloud cover obscures our view. Ward is disappointed, but not heartbroken. He's missed the Northern Lights twice because of rainy days.

After stopping for lemon shake-ups, our group ventures through the community park on our way to the woods, where we hope to enjoy an hour of this fine day surrounded by greenery. In the park, we see a full variety of characters. Doomsdayers, drunken college students, science geeks, religious groups, and family picnics are all present within a quarter-mile radius. They each approach the day with vastly different agendas. Parents pester their children to take an interest in the event, but most of the younger children appear to be clueless about the day's significance. One group huddles around a man who elevates himself on a hill, reading scripture to a crowd. A verse from *Revelations*, I assume. The college kids shamelessly chug beers, leaving their cans wherever they finish them. A couple of the kids are throwing a frisbee without regard for any of the other patrons trying to enjoy their day. In the few minutes we've been here, I've witnessed their frisbee land in two separate family picnics. If their frisbee comes anywhere near my group, I swear I'm going to fling it line drive, deep into the thicket.

Sitting alone on a park bench, staring at the clouds that shroud the sun, a man in a full-length Egyptian garb and golden headdress is whispering to himself. He has a hooked staff in one hand and he holds what appears to be a religious text in the other. I tell the group that I'm going to go speak with him, secretly hoping they'll talk me out of it. Instead I receive sincere support and encouragement.

"Go ahead, take as long as you need," says Wendy. "We'll be right here."

As a young writer, I'm often burdened by my supporting friends and family who bolster me into action, even when the task is beyond my comfort zone. I'd rather speculate about the man and continue to use humor as a defense mechanism to avoid my fear of speaking with him, but with all eyes on me, there's no backing out. I wander toward the man and introduce myself as a journalist with a human interest magazine called *The Decaturian* (the campus newspaper at my college, Millikin University), and reach out my hand to shake his. The man takes his eyes off the sky for a second to respectfully nod, then returns his attention to the sun. Now that I'm up close, his eclipse glasses coupled with his robe make him look like a space age prophet. I have no idea what he believes, why he's dressed in this fashion, or even what his name is, but I already sense his mystic charisma. Despite the scientific foundation of my beliefs, his allure pulls me at the core. He is truly magnetic.

"What's your name, sir?"

"Elijah," he says as the clouds finally part.

I put on my glasses and we stare at the sun in silence. Currently, it's only about 3/4ths visible. Its moon phase equivalent is a waxing gibbous. Seeing this preview while in the company of this mystic instantly loosens my inhibitions. It's at least a full minute before I remember to ask for an interview.

"What would you like to know?"

What would I like to know? I have no idea. Usually when I interview strangers, the questions rise organically, but this time, my mind is blank.

"Whatever you'd like to share," I reply.

We remain silent for another full minute. Apparently, the only thing worth sharing is the moment itself. His reticence isn't rude, it's enchanting. Elijah isn't stoic; the smile on his face resembles the sun itself. My posture is better than ever. Elijah's mere presence is realigning my spine. I look at the book in his hand. It's a leather-bound copy of *The Egyptian Book of the Dead*. Shifting back to the sun, we watch it drifting further behind the moon. Elijah breaks into laughter, but doesn't say a word. My primitive brain naturally associates his wardrobe and demeanor with the movement of the sun, but this illogical association is promptly overridden by my knowledge of David Hume. I suppose it doesn't take a philosopher to point out the preposterous attributes of this association, but this mental lag is making me more sympathetic to those who often buy into these types of logical fallacies. Not everyone has access to the work of Hume. In the beginning of this story, I myself support a logical fallacy known as *Appeal to Authority* by affirming Ward as a "genius" based on the firm handshake he received from the well-known genius, Neil deGrasse Tyson. Although Ward may very well be a genius, his mere association with Mr. Tyson does not qualify him for this adjective. I've had the luxury of higher education, I've dedicated countless hours of my spare time toward learning how to approach the world in the most logical way possible. Yet I'm still prone to buying and shilling these basic logical fallacies.

My monkey brain wants to drop my pen, hurl my notebook in the trash, strip my clothes, and exchange them for a garb. I want to drop to my knees and praise Ra, the sun god. In another life, I could be an Inca warrior, beating animal skin drums in celebration of a sacrifice. I could be a Baptist minister, hanging warning signs about the apocalypse, or a carnie, using the eclipse as an opportunity to capitalize. I could be a frat boy, drinking canned beer in my BRO-BIDEN tank top. Here I am now, half-tempted to buy whatever Elijah isn't even selling. For all I know, he's just an ordinary guy with a passion for black robes and ancient Egypt.

"You know," he finally speaks, "this is a special day. The sun, it shines high above us. It provides the energy needed for all life on Earth. If there's one thing I have in common with you, with the squirrels, with the grass beneath our
     feet, it's that without the sun, we'd all be dust."

I don't think he's talking about the eclipse. After a soft "Yeah," we sit in silence for another minute or so, before I thank him for the interview and catch up with my friends. They joke about Elijah, calling him the pharaoh of Shawnee Forest, a national park in southern Illinois.

I laugh along, while watching the grass glow green in the sunlight.

12:27 P.M.

Meteorology is my scientific specialty. I can forecast the weather days in advance solely by observing cloud patterns. Thick stratus or cumulus clouds tell us that precipitation is likely in the following days. A lack of clouds tells us the upcoming weather will be fair. Today the overcast stratocumulus clouds that blot out 2/3rds of the sky tell me there's a high % chance of this expedition being fucked. We're in the forest now, and once again the world is cast in a tint of dreary grey. Despite the gloom, Wendy, Griffin, and Emma sing an upbeat campfiresque song that I am unfamiliar with. I try to record the lyrics, but the group harasses me into closing my notebook for a moment to "just hangout." The group keeps singing and my mind drifts into more speculation as I try to imagine what Wendy's life has become. Wendy and I knew each other mostly in adolescence, when we wore primarily black and sat in the far back corner of the gymnasium, stealing swigs of her dad's whiskey during high school dances and making fun of the popular kids. What clichés we were. But look at her now, singing and skipping with the beauty and the brawn, while I trail behind and try to conceive spiteful remarks to scrawl for my literary gonzo exposé. I suppose she grew up and learned to embrace the world, while my snarky cynicism shifted toward a different kind of cliché, one that's a little more vogue.

Griffin is a true beefcake. I want to hate him, but he's funny, kind, inquisitive, and has been more than welcoming to both Ward and I. I don't want to like Emma either, but I can honestly say that she shares all the same virtues that I listed for Griffin. My whining, high school self feels betrayed that Wendy hangs out with the cool kids, but deeper inside I'm proud that she's made friends with Emma and Griffin. They're not just the classic depiction of what it means to be cool, they're actually enjoyable to be around.

Sometime during my reflection, the singing stopped and the group split into two separate conversations. Wendy and Emma talk about music. They're discussing the work of a band called *Dirty Art Club*, an experimental group who compose instrumental pieces that are a hybrid between jazz rock and new age psychedelic electronica. Hearing this, I realize that I've misjudged Emma once again. Not that there's anything wrong with this, but I had assumed that she listened to top twenty artists like Katy Perry or whatever they play at the parties I'm not invited too.

As I eavesdrop further, I discover that my assumption is far from reality. Emma's dream after college is to open an Indie Rock club that features chic artists with mostly niche followings. She invokes the same hipster musicians that I get made fun of for listening too, such as *King Krule, My Morning Jacket, Hiatus Kaiyote,* and *Tune-Yards.* How could I have been so blind? What color is Emma's top? Black. I know nothing about Emma. Who was she in high school? Is she even from a small town as I'd so confidently presumed earlier? Who is this girl? Who is Griffin for that matter? He and Ward are deep in conversation. They're talking about science, but not physics, biology. Griffin speaks with such confidence that over Ward's shoulder, I can tell we're sharing revelation as we both realize that must be his major.

Griffin is telling Ward about an invasive flower to the Shawnee National Forest that resembles another flower, a common snack in the diet of deer and other local wildlife. However, this new invasive flower is poisonous and has been killing the animals who eat it. Although the animals are beginning to catch on, they cannot tell the difference between the poisonous plant and the plant they're used to eating, so most of the animals are willing to take the gamble. It's fascinating stuff. Griffin points out one of the flowers and says that even he, a trained biologist, cannot tell the difference. Ward asks him what the odds are, because he's getting kind of hungry. I should probably add one more attribute to Griffin's stat sheet: intelligent.

12:53 P.M.

We're at the edge of the woods now. The trail we've been following has taken us full circle. Soon, we'll be back on the SIU campus. A megaphone in the distance announces that totality is in exactly half an hour. The crowd is concealed by a prairie grass thicket, but we can sure hear them cheer. Ward and I both smile.

We're happy to know that so many people are excited for this phenomenon. Listening to their uproar while walking through a gap where the yellow grass opens, we're induced with group elation like high school football players storming the tunnel before a homecoming game. As we reach the clearing, the sun returns. I ask Ward if, based on the current cloud situation, he thinks we'll be able to see totality.

"Only time will tell," he says. "Only time will tell."

1:00 P.M.

Three clouds on the western side of the sky converge to form a giant stratocumulus cloud, and this super-cloud drifts directly in front of the sun. Despite that we're likely wasting our time, we search for a place to view totality. We still have twenty minutes, and if we pick any direction (aside from back into the woods) and walk continuously, we'll still technically be a part of the same crowd we're in now. We decide that here is as good of a spot as any, but we might as well roam around for a minute in search of a place to sit. After meandering for a bit, it appears that all seats have been taken. Wendy has a blanket in her backpack, but the only open patch of grass within sight is isolated by wires and caution tape that quarantine some high-tech science equipment. Whatever the equipment is, it must be important, as its operators are frantic anytime a passerby so much as brushes the tape, which piques the curiosity of both Ward and I. So we decide to investigate.

As we approach their tent, the equipment's operators stand up and squabble toward us, waving their arms and shouting in a frenzy. Ward starts to reverse, but quick on my feet, I pull out my Millikin student ID and present it as a press pass, saying, "It's okay, I'm here in an official journalistic capacity!" Hearing that I am a journalist, their tone immediately changes from accusatory to apologetic. They inquire about my publication, and I inform them that I'm with *The Decaturian*, a scientific journal based out of Decatur, IL. The operators apologize one last time. They warn us to step softly because their equipment is hypersensitive to vibrations, then they retreat from the tape to find their supervisor.

I can't believe my tomfoolery worked, but I adjust my collar with confidence and do my best to maintain the illusion that I'm supposed to be doing this. The supervisor is an Indian woman, probably in her fifties. She keeps working as she speaks with us, scribbling figures in a notebook. She introduces herself, but due to her thick accent, in tandem with my untrained ear, I have to ask her to repeat herself thrice before she finally hands me a business card. Padma Yanamandra is her name. She's the leader of a research team for the PACA (Professional-Amateur Collaborative Astronomy) project, here collecting data that will be used by NASA to read the temperature of the sun's corona.

"We have a match work of sixty-eight identical telescopes set up at locations where the eclipse will reach totality between Oregon and South Carolina," she says before I ask a question. "We are using a 'K-Way' telescope, but we have modified it by adding a polar measure to the camera. The reason being, we are interested in understanding how and why the corona increases in temperature away from the sun as opposed to dropping in temperature."

This is the only quotation I'm going to include from this interview, because the next seventeen minutes of discussion involve her and Ward playing intellectual tennis while I retrieve their balls. I want to use her thick accent as an excuse for my lack of understanding, but Ward comprehends her just fine. While they discuss, I nod attentively, while sketching a doodle of the U.S.S. Phallic flying into a dyonic black hole. Once I've added the stars, I flip to a new page and draw an illustration of Padma, Ward, and a group of extraterrestrials abducting me from a cow patty. I frequently look up as I sketch to present the appearance that I'm taking detailed notes. This justifies why the conduction of this interview is a two-man job.

Ward and Padma are communicating on another frequency. If they continue much longer, they'll transcend oral language and converse via telepathy. Trying to restore my place in the conversation, my eyes dart back and forth between brain and brain, but the harder I try to focus, the more I'm lost among the stars. For the first time today, for the first time in a long time, I feel intellectually inadequate.

Padma ends the interview abruptly and apologetically, as she and her team must double-check their equipment before totality. Ward and I thank her for the interview, then return to our group, who are patiently staring at the clouds. The same voice from earlier announces that we are five minutes from totality and that we should keep our eclipse glasses on until further notice. But currently, our glasses are unnecessary, as the eclipse is still shrouded by the tail end of the aforementioned super-cloud. The cloud is moving quickly and is likely to drift out of the sun's way. However, another cloud trails near behind, floating at the same pace. Once again, I ask Ward for the probability. He tells me to chill out, and guesstimates that our odds are 40/60.

"40/60!" I groan in a way that's accusatory of both Ward and Mother Nature.

Wendy sarcastically mimics my groan, which I greatly appreciate. Being in each other's presence causes us both to revert to our immature high-schoolish mannerisms and mindset. All day, we have been children.

"That's just how these things go," says Ward, bringing us back to adulthood.

The megaphone voice belts out once again, "Two minutes until totality."

This announcement is followed by whoops and cheers. The vibe around here is like the line at an amusement park. The crowd is a mix of people who'd never congregate under ordinary circumstances. Everybody is sweaty, stinky, and greased with oily sunscreen. They're all buying tacky carnival junk and sugary beverages. We're all excited for something that will be short-lived and may not even happen. It's 95° degrees. In the crowd, it's at least 105°. A half-drunk bozo who's yanking three kids around bumps my right shoulder three times and never apologizes. Now I understand why murder rates are directly correlated with the heat index. Why the hell did I wear jeans today? It's like my pants are filled with hot glue. Bump. If this guy bumps me again, I'm going to volunteer him for a human sacrifice.

The megaphone belts out again, "One minute until totality!"

The crowd erupts. The supercloud still blocks our view, but could open up at any second. Ward taps his foot to a thrash-metal beat. Katie has her phone out, ready to record the first ten seconds of the phenomenon for all her friends on Snapchat. Just past Ward, Griffin reaches out for Wendy's hand. As she offers it, he takes hold, raises it to his mouth, and kisses her ever-so gently. For Fuck's sake, that was charming. My eyelid twitches. I am tweaking out.

1:22 P.M.

The cloud parts as the megaphone operator announces, "Totality is here." The sky goes dark. More navy blue than black, but dark enough to see stars all the way across the horizon. Birds stop chirping. The squirrels withdraw to their trees. Insects hum like it's the middle of the night. The crowd goes bananas. It's the most excitable cheering I've heard since the Chicago Cubs won the World Series. Everybody's hugging. I jump at Ward and he catches me in midair. He looks like he might cry. I might cry. The bozo to my right bumps me again and I don't even care. I pat him on the shoulder and he nods to me, raising his youngest child to the sky like a newborn king. I take off my glasses and stare at the eclipse.

The sun's corona glows around the moon like a halo. Seeing it this way, our home star appears to have doubled in size. The day-time sky sprinkled with stars; the thousands of people marveling at this naturally occurring event; the big ball of flaming gas, burning behind the moon, providing the fuel for all life on Earth; the big stupid smile slapped on Ward's face; this is one of the most beautiful moments I've ever been a part of. I hug Wendy. I hug Emma. I even hug Griffin.

Then we all circle together for one massive group hug.

Looking at Ward again, I can never tell what's going on inside his cranium. It may just be pure awe, but whatever he's thinking, it's certainly profound. Emma is loosely holding her cellphone at waist height. I think she forgot to record a Snapchat. Instead, she glows, splaying her arms, legs, and fingers, letting 100 Billion neutrinos pass through every square centimeter of her body. I get the impression that she knows they're passing through her. She may not know what a neutrino is, but she's in line with the moon and the sun, and can feel the sun's energy penetrating her skin.

Griffin and Wendy are making out. No one in the crowd seems to be bothered by this, not even me. I even let out a sarcastically romantic whistle. A few religious people raise their hands and sing a hymn in praise. Padma and her employees take turns gazing through their fancy telescope; each one of them in tears. A few stoners pass a joint amongst themselves, giggling and squinting at the day-time stars. Even the carnies stop frying their funnel cakes long enough to inhale the spirit. Everyone in this vast crowd of people is having their own, equally profound moments of ecstasy. I have no idea what's going on in any of their heads, or in any of their lives. Frankly, it's none of my business. All the effort I've spent looking down on people today was a misplacement of my energy. I am a hypocrite, not because I contradict myself, but because I judge others for reflecting my flaws. Hypocrisy doesn't exist because individuals have conflicting ideas and emotions. Each momentary perception is a part of the true self. Hypocrisy only exists when contradiction and judgment are in tandem. It's okay to have inconsistencies, but looking down is a rude, unproductive way of looking in.

Now the horizon burns orange. The sun slowly floats away from the moon, casting a beam of light on the Earth. As it drifts, the crowd lets out a collective holler as though descending from the peak of a roller coaster.

The megaphone announces, "Please, reinstate your protective eyewear. Thank you."

The sky brightens up. Apollo and Luna finally part. The Earth glows with a post-coital bliss, but only for a moment, as the now-partial eclipse is consumed by the clouds.

2:05 P.M.

Our group decides to stop for late-lunch before Ward and I get back on the road. We order veggie burgers at a basement bar called *The Underground*. Wendy and Griffin share one side of the booth, while Emma and I make a Ward sandwich on the other. I secure my wall seat by claiming I need elbow space to write, but really, I'm adding the final touches to the U.S.S. Phallic.

We each order a celebratory beer. There's a smile plastered on each one of our faces. For the first time today, we look like a full group rather than three cool cats followed by a couple misfits. We're all starving, and due to the post-eclipse rush, it's clearly going to be awhile before we get our food. I pull out the rest of my gummy bears and share them with the table. Ward and I chew them whole, but the others chomp the heads first.

3:34 P.M.

Ward and I have parted ways with the entourage. We shared hugs, shared laughs, but we did not share phone numbers. Emma and Griffin, I will never meet them again.

Ward and I are stuck in a traffic jam at the edge of Carbondale. It will be at least an hour before we reach city limits. We've been in the car for fifteen minutes, and he has already reverted to fun facts.

"Did you know that the sun is 4.5 billion years old and has burned nearly half of its hydrogen supply?" he says. "In another 5 billion years, after all the hydrogen has been burned, it will expand, engulfing Mercury, Venus, and Earth. At that point, it'll be considered a red giant, but as of now, it's a main-sequence G2V star, otherwise known as a yellow dwarf."

I'm too busy reviewing my notes to comment on how the sun, the source of all known life, will eventually infanticize its own children in a cannibalistic fashion. I smile and nod without looking up from my notes. Suddenly, Ward slams on the breaks, as the two cars in front of us collide bumper to bumper. We stay put until both drivers get out to exchange insurance information. The fun facts, the fender bender... I'm suffering severe déjà vu. The juxtaposition is too perfect, as if the stars have aligned to provide the perfect closer for this self-reflective exposé. We pull forward a bit and I see a license plate rattling in the street. Another layer of coincidence, so strange I almost puke. Mississippi, make that twenty-seven.

Reference

Webmaster Blogger. (2010, November 11). *MBTI self-assessment essay.* Hot Essays. Retrieved from hotessays.blogspot.com

CHAPTER 7

The Great Wall of Insanity

J. M. Spence

Arriving at the prison was very much what I expected. My writing professor and I pulled up to a mostly empty parking lot on a cold, wet Saturday morning. We signed in with a guard, walked through a metal detector, and waited for someone to escort us through several sets of steel doors. The building had previously been a psychiatric facility, so it was all thick white doors instead of bars. An officer checked our shoes and led us through another door. We would be visiting throughout the semester to meet with a small group of women in an effort to help them tell their critical stories.

While the facility's facade fits all the cliché stereotypes of a low minimum-security correctional center for women, walking in with my college professor wasn't the way I had imagined myself going to prison. The first time I was brought home by the police, I was six years old. My grandmother had gifted me a children's atlas earlier that day. The atlas devoted two entire pages to the Great Wall of China. As far as I could tell, the Great Wall of China was just on the other side of the lake (oceans and lakes are the same thing to a six-year-old), and I had been to the other side of the lake before. I decided I would visit the Great Wall of China. I made it about three blocks before an older couple stopped me to ask what I was doing. As I excitedly explained that I was going to China, the guy sat outside listening while his wife went inside. A few minutes later a police officer pulled up. The officer told me I couldn't go to China and that he would be taking me home. He showed me some of the cool technology in the front of his car and let me talk on the radio before he walked me up to my front door. My mom beat my ass when he left.

I was fourteen the first time I got expelled from school. On the first day of high school gym class, we were given a Master lock and told to go to the locker rooms and pick a locker. A group of girls cornered me in the locker room and made slurs about my sexuality. One girl threw her padlock at me. She missed. I didn't tell the teacher that the other girls were mean, that they'd tried to physically assault me. I told her that if she made me go back to the locker room, I'd kill everyone. I spent a week in a psychiatric facility for that comment. I had been taking antidepressants since the 7th grade. This time, they determined that I was bipolar and changed my medication. This started a cascade of diagnoses and medication changes that would go on for the remainder of my teen years: depression, anxiety, bipolar disorder, ADHD, borderline personality disorder, and possibly an autism spectrum disorder.

In order for me to be allowed back in school, my parents had to consent to having me placed in a special education program. I didn't get a say, so I became a special education student. My behavior only worsened. I wasn't being bullied any less, and now I was bored, too. I was also heavily medicated. I spent my mornings disrupting whichever class I was in and usually went home before noon. The school approved of my leaving midday, if nothing else, to prevent further disruption to other students.

By the end of my sophomore year, I had been expelled from the special ed program. I had also completed six separate inpatient visits to various psychiatric facilities across the state, including a four month stay at Choate Mental Health Center, formerly known as the Southern Hospital for the Insane.

• • •

Built in 1869, Choate sits on over 300 acres, has six living areas, an administrative building, a school, a gym, a swimming pool, and a cemetery. Presently, it houses around two-hundred people, from adolescents to adults, found not guilty by reason of insanity in a court of law.

I stayed on the adolescent unit, called Redbud, which had a day room/dining room area, about fifteen double-person bedrooms, and a nurses' station. The dining room area included all of the amenities typically found in a kitchen, as we were responsible for preparing our own meals. I lived at Choate for about three hours before I started getting into trouble. Psychiatric medication, especially mood stabilizers and antipsychotics, often causes weight gain. At 5'7, I weighed 215 pounds. Blood tests indicated that my triglycerides, the amount of fat in my blood, were three times as high as they should have been. The nutritionist put me on a diet.

For dinner the first night, Redbud was sent off-brand pizza hot pockets. I was told that they weren't part of my diet and was instead given a cup of unflavored yogurt. After dinner, it was decided that my chore for the day would be washing dishes. For the food I didn't get to eat. I didn't do any dishes that night. Instead, I threatened a staffer with a fork from the sink. Staff took away silverware from everyone for a week, and we all had to eat with plastic spoons. This didn't earn me any friends.

I had another food-related incident not long after. It was my night to cook. I made tuna casserole and boiled brussels sprouts because those are the ingredients we were sent. I wasn't allowed to eat the pasta, which I didn't find out until after I had made it, but staff told me I could have as many brussels sprouts as

I wanted. Despite hating cabbage in all forms, I was so hungry that I ate three plates of brussels sprouts. I spent all night throwing up brussels sprouts, and I haven't eaten one since. My roommate didn't make my situation at Choate any better. Kim was a blonde girl, about my age, with a propensity for picking fights. In the evenings, she liked to throw things at me and shout that I needed to stop throwing things at her. I think she hoped that I would be scolded, but all the staff ever did was tell her to be quiet. One evening, after a trip to the gym, during which she intentionally hit me in the back of the head with a football, she was throwing puzzle pieces at me from across the dayroom. The two staff members in the room ignored it, probably because she was throwing the pieces quietly. I jumped up and stepped into her personal space. I told her that I was done having things thrown at me. One of the staff members finally got up to stop the impending fight, but the other told him to back off. "Let them fight," said the other staffer, a large blonde woman named Debbie. Kim pushed me. I pushed back. I punched her in the face and the staff pulled us apart. I separated easily, put my hands up and sat down at the dining room table. Kim lost her shit. She tried to fight with the staff and ended up in restraints. The next day, a morning staffer told me how disappointed she was that I engaged with Kim in the first place. She said Kim couldn't help it because of her severely low IQ, but that I should have known better.

After an incident with another patient, I was put on a 1:1 restriction, which meant that a staff member must be within 10 feet of me at all times. The staff member was also to take notes on what I was doing every 15 minutes, 24 hours a day. This included watching me in the bathroom and in the shower. When I refused to use the bathroom, the nurse set up a plan that said I was not to be fed until I drank 4 ounces of prune juice. This went on for over a week. Unfortunately, bodily processes eventually surpass willpower. Although my 1:1 plan only required one staff member at my side at all times, Debbie decided she also wanted to be present to witness the impending horror. It was every bit as humiliating as one would imagine.

The shower situation had come to a head first, though, when after three or four days without bathing someone woke me up in the middle of the night. I was escorted to the shower room, a tiled room with four back-to-back stalls, eight in total, and two drains, one on each side. I wouldn't strip so three staff members I didn't know put me on the floor and took my clothes off. They dragged me to one of the stalls and turned the water on. It was freezing. One of them squirted me with a bottle of dish soap, and they simply stood there and told me to rinse off.

Afterwards, they gave me a glass of prune juice and sent me back to bed. Despite all of this, the most unpleasant thing I experienced at Choate was their idea of punishment. They couldn't beat us, so they punished us in other ways. Debbie's favorite method of punishment was, in my opinion, the hardest to deal with. Any time I was being difficult, she would have the nurse order me a dose of the antipsychotic Haldol. Haldol is known to cause extrapyramidal symptoms (EPS) such as muscle contractions, tremors, involuntary jerking or twitching, motor restlessness, and Parkinson-like symptoms. A double-blind study on Haldol indicated that 50% of subjects who received the drug experienced at least one extrapyramidal symptom. While they're not actually life-threatening, they're far more unpleasant to endure than they sound. The Wikipedia page for motor restlessness (akathisia) lists a single complication: suicide.

Haldol, as an antipsychotic, is meant to shut down delusions. It's strong as fuck. People who do not take the drug regularly do not build up a tolerance, and within ten minutes of injection you're drooling on yourself. The only thing you can do is sleep. I'm also one of the 50% of people to get Haldol-induced EPS. The feeling is incredibly hard to describe and even harder to experience. I get a desperate sense of needing to tear open my chest and crawl out of my body while simultaneously being too exhausted to move. It makes breathing more difficult than it should be. It would probably cause a panic attack if it didn't make me too tired to hyperventilate.

But this was not enough for Debbie. Giving out antipsychotics as punishment was apparently not punishment enough. Once given the shot, Debbie would have me sit in a chair near the door of the dayroom. If I would start to fall asleep, she'd make me stand up. Sometimes I would fall and she would have to help me up. Then she would make me do jumping jacks in sets of 20 until I was alert enough that I was doing them properly. At that point, she would make me sit back down and again wait until I was falling asleep before starting the process over. She would do this for about an hour before sending me to my room and letting me sleep off the remainder of the 12 hours of Haldol's potency.

• • •

By the time I left Choate, four months after arriving, I felt like I had been there for years. Every second of Haldol Jumping Jacks is an absolute eternity. I somehow managed to both avoid being sent back to Choate and graduate high school. I hadn't considered college, but for some reason the community college offered me a full scholarship. I failed classes for three semesters before dropping out. I got a job at a manufacturing plant, when my girlfriend unexpectedly informed me that she was pregnant. I rented an apartment, worked, and took care of her kid. I was under the impression I was becoming an actual adult, but, like everything else, it didn't last.

After two years, my girlfriend changed up her regular disappearing act by coming home after a week with no word with the name "Tracey" tattooed on her neck. She said she was taking our son and moving to Wisconsin with a woman she had just met, who, pointedly, was not named Tracey. Two days before Christmas, I was laid off from the manufacturing plant. I got a job handing out free samples in a large retail store. Standing in one place all day was hard for me, but my boss took my inattention for initiative, and I was promoted to lead after two months. At one point, my boss decided to fire an employee for making a rude comment to a guest. He informed me that I'd be the one to deliver the news. For some reason, my 21-year-old self didn't find it inappropriate to conclude the separation with an offer of drinks. To my surprise, she accepted. She came over a few nights later and stayed for five years. We moved to Los Angeles, where she's from, until the relationship came to a crashing end.

• • •

I had a difficult time moving forward, once I got back to Illinois. I didn't have anywhere to go, so I moved in with my parents. My first night there, I laid on a mattress in their basement and played a movie on my laptop. For the most part, I didn't get up for over a year.

I spent a lot of time contemplating suicide and eventually settled on an overdose of antidepressants. Based on the research I had done; a week's worth would be enough to kill me. I would fall asleep and stop breathing. It seemed about as painless as death could be. I took a 30-day supply one-by-one. I had eaten almost all of them when my dad walked into my room, something he almost never does.

We were at the emergency room in five minutes flat. My dad told the person at the front desk what had happened, and they walked us directly into triage. The next thing I knew I was waking up in ICU. I had a thick plastic tube down my throat and the left side of my face was covered in black goo. When the nurses took the tube out, one of them apologized for the mess. "I tried to clean you up last night," she told me. I asked what happened. Apparently in the ER they had given me activated charcoal to make me vomit up the antidepressants. I lost consciousness after drinking the solution and threw up all over myself. I guess the nurses would clean me up and then I would do it again. At one point, I aspirated vomit and at another I stopped breathing altogether. They had to intubate me.

• • •

I was mostly in a daze following my suicide attempt. I was angry that I had been interrupted and "saved." I didn't want to be saved. I wanted to be done. I started using drugs whenever they were available. My preference was simply to not be sober. After I had been smoking synthetic marijuana for a while, I became delusional upon withdrawal.

I called the local mental health center twice, but they were getting frustrated with the mania that had clearly set in and my complete lack of logical thought. They hung up on me both times. I tried going to the emergency room, but they sent me away. When I went home, I had a minor argument with a neighbor and responded by taking a baseball bat to the windows of the neighbor's house. I was arrested for damage to property but paid the $100 bail immediately. The next day, I called the mental health center again and asked if I needed to make a bomb threat to get them to listen to me. They informed the police, as required by law, but the police made the determination that I wasn't an actual danger.

I broke the neighbor's windows on a Thursday and it wasn't until the next Tuesday that the police finally decided to do a welfare check. I ranted about crystals coming out of a woman's skin but, otherwise, insisted I was "fine, now." I hadn't slept in over a week by this point. The officers placed me on a 72-hour mental health hold and took me to the psychiatric unit at the local hospital.

It took 12 hours to complete my admission to the unit, and, once they finally did, a nurse gave me a shot of an anti-anxiety drug, hoping it would help me calm down and hopefully sleep. Instead, my whole body started shaking. The nurses told me to "stop fighting it," as if I would suddenly see logic and relax. I went to my room, still shaking, and after a few minutes there were a dozen nurses at the door to give me a Haldol injection. I let them give me the shot, but it didn't stop the shaking. They decided I should be restrained for my own safety.

When two nurses rolled in a bed with straps on it, I bolted for the door. I wasn't having any logical thoughts. If I was, I would have known that I was on a locked unit with nowhere to run. There were still a dozen nurses in my room when this happened. I got to the doorway and they tackled me like I played for the NFL. All of my limbs flailed as I tried to keep my balance. My back hit the floor at the same time both of my feet connected with a nurse's chest. The security guard, who was on the floor struggling with me, called out, "that's assault!" as he sprayed mace in my eyes from about 3 inches away. I was arrested from the psychiatric unit.

This is a common occurrence. There are ten times more Americans with a debilitating mental illness in prison or jail than in a treatment facility. 2 million people with a mental illness are arrested each year and they make up 15–30% of jail inmates. 83% of those people have no access to treatment.

At the police station, I was fingerprinted, and my picture was taken. I had no bond until I went in front of a judge. I was told to change into blue scrubs, but the officer stopped me halfway through. She said my underwear, boxers, which I always wear, were considered shorts because I'm female. She made me take them off. My bra had an underwire. She took it, too.

I was handed a wool blanket, a towel, a washcloth, and a pair of orange rubber sandals. The officer had me put them in a plastic bin. I was also handed what looked like a giant plastic tarp and told to carry the items to my pod. There were two tables in the middle of the room, a shower with a toilet/sink combo on each side near the door, and eight sets of metal bunk bed frames lining the walls further back. I was directed to my bed, on the top bunk. Apparently, the tarp-like monstrosity was supposed to be a mattress. I stretched it out over the steel frame and climbed up. The medication had kicked in, so I slept easily.

A tall blonde woman woke me up and shoved a styrofoam cup in my face. She was another inmate. "Drink this," she told me. I reached out for the cup with one hand. It seemed to be water. I took a sip and tried to hand it back to her. She stood there and had me drink all of it. Eventually I handed her the empty cup and went back to sleep.

She kept waking me up, handing me water and waiting for me to drink it. She asked about my washcloth. She wet it and put it on my forehead. She kept asking if I was okay. I nodded and went back to sleep. Apparently, we did this for a few days. She later admitted that she was mostly just making sure I was still alive. I wasn't getting my medication while I was in jail. When I went to court, the judge set my bail at $10,000. This meant I had to pay $1,000 to be released, of which I had nothing. I filled out a request form to see the doctor. I knew my case manager at the mental health clinic had brought all my medication to the jail. The doctor had changed all my prescriptions, despite never seeing me once. I wasn't getting any better.

After two weeks, I started menstruating. I still didn't have any underwear. I panicked. I tried to discreetly explain my situation to one of the correctional officers, but I was hyperventilating. She didn't understand what I was saying and seemed to quickly get frustrated. After less than two minutes talking to me she just walked away and shut the steel door of the pod. I went back to my bunk and tried not to cry, still hyperventilating.

It was lights out and the woman on the top bunk across from mine started huffing and tossing in bed every time I gasped for air. I mumbled out a quick apology and tried to suffocate more quietly. My gasping didn't stop and neither did her huffing. She made snarky comments but that failed to help me breathe. She told me to shut up and that, too, had no effect. I had eventually heard enough and told her to fuck off.

She tried to goad me into a fight. I said I wasn't interested. I got out of my bunk and started pacing around the tables in the center of the room. A CO called over the loudspeaker and told me to get back in my bunk. I tried to explain the situation, and she said she didn't care. I went back to pacing but the next time the voice on the loudspeaker told me to get back in my bunk, I complied. I was still hyperventilating.

The woman went back to taunting me. I jumped down from my bunk, grabbed a plastic spoon that was on a desk between the bunks, and climbed up the bunk across from mine. I accidentally stepped on the person lying on the bottom bunk as I brought the bottom end of the spoon down hard toward the face of the woman taunting me. It connected with her cheek and folded uselessly. The woman pushed me back just far enough to kick me in the face. I tried going at her a few more times but couldn't get the leverage I needed. She kept kicking me in the face, and I kept going back. Eventually I saw the remote to the television on the desk and grabbed it. I threw it at her. She ducked, and it hit the wall, shattering. It was about this time that two CO's entered the room with handcuffs out. I stepped up against the wall and put my hands up.

• • •

They put me on suicide watch, which meant I had to wear a thick velcro vest over an otherwise naked body. I told the female CO that I was bleeding, and she said she didn't care. I didn't like the indignity of bleeding all over myself with no way to stop it, but since I knew that didn't matter to her, I tried explaining that it was unsanitary to bleed all over something that someone else was going to have to wear. It wasn't until I lied and told her I have HIV that she paused.

Her male supervisor knocked at the door and asked if everything was going okay. I guess we had been in there awhile. As soon as I mentioned the word 'period' he told the CO with me that I could have underwear and a sanitary pad. That was all I needed in the first place, but, despite the fight for my dignity and my life, I was grateful to finally get it.

Suicide watch placement is in a holding cell. The mental health professional said that the doctor ordered for me to remain on suicide watch until he was able to visit me but that he would be on vacation for the next five days. He still had not approved my prescribed medication. The woman from mental health told me that she was trying to get me transferred to a psychiatric facility but, seeing as I was arrested from one, she was having trouble getting a place to take me.

I was humiliated, disrespected, called a "crazy bitch" by a guard who never once spoke to me, kept virtually naked in a small box for days on end, and refused medical treatment. More appalling, though, was knowing that these incidents were not isolated, that inmates all over the country were experiencing similar or worse treatment. Entire state justice departments have recently been sued for inadequate medical and mental health care, as well as for excessive use of solitary confinement.

I was in the 8x10' holding cell for three days before I was released for an hour of exercise. I asked if I could place a phone call and the CO agreed. I called my parents. I cried as I explained the situation I was in. My dad said he wasn't sure I had learned my lesson. I had no confirmation one way or the other about whether my parents would help me when I was led back to my cell. My dad picked me up an hour later, and I found it odd to feel so deeply thankful and ashamed at the same time.

• • •

The felony assault charge was dropped in exchange for pleading guilty to breaking the neighbor's windows, a misdemeanor. As part of my probation, I was to attend school or work. I had forgotten school was an option and since I didn't have any real work qualifications, I figured I may as well try again. I graduated with honors from the community college I had previously dropped out of. I finished substance abuse therapy and completed my probation. I have one year left of university, where I'm a psychology major with a biology minor, and I'm currently looking at graduate schools. I hope to be accepted into a behavioral neuroscience program, so I can earn a PhD and conduct research on the physical attributes of psychiatric illnesses. I would like to find better ways to help people like myself, who struggle with mental health problems, to manage their conditions.

Unfortunately, in Illinois, the state in which I live, mental health care has been increasingly difficult to obtain. Since 2009, mental health services in Illinois have received hundreds of millions of dollars in budget cuts leaving social service agencies throughout the state unpaid and unable to keep their doors open. Instead, the people who desperately need those services end up in jail or in prison rather than getting help.

I was incredibly lucky to have a regular mental health care provider as well as family and other social support. Without them, I'd probably be another statistic in one of our country's many problems with the prison system, caught in an endless cycle of behavioral problems and incarceration exacerbated by lack of appropriate and accessible mental health care. Many aren't so lucky. State and federal funding for mental health care is not adequate. It is mostly due to the help I received that I was able to avoid prison and am on my way to becoming a productive member of society. With better mental health funding and services, we could prevent others from being caught up in that cycle.

References

Alfano, A. (2015). Many psychiatric drugs have serious effects on body weight. *Scientific American.* Retrieved from www.scientificamerican.com/article/many-psychiatric-drugs-have-serious-effects-on-body-w eight/

American Civil Liberties Union. (2012, March 6). *Lawsuit charges Arizona prison officials with failing to provide adequate health care, inhumane use of solitary confinement.* Retrieved from www.aclu.org/news/lawsuit-charges-arizona-prison-officials-failing-provide-adequate-health -care-inhumane-use

Anna State Hospital. (n.d.) *Asylum projects.* Retrieved from www.asylumprojects.org/index.php/Anna_State_Hospital

Kadner, P. (2015, May 29). Report: Mental health care in crisis in Illinois. *The Chicago Tribune.* Retrieved from www.chicagotribune.com/suburbs/daily-southtown/opinion/ct-sta-kadner-mental-st-0529 -20150528-story.html

Liebelson, D. (2017, June 24). He had fresh head injuries': What Ohio has been doing to mentally ill boys. *Mother Jones.* Retrieved from www.motherjones.com/politics/2014/04/doj-solitary-confinement-mentally-ill-children-ohio/

Melville, N. A. (2013, December 12). Synthetic cannabis triggers 'Spiceophrenia'. *Medscape.* Retrieved from www.medscape.com/viewarticle/817745

National Alliance on Mental Illness. (n.d.). *Jailing people with mental illness.* Retrieved from www.nami.org/learn-more/public-policy/jailing-people-with-mental-illness

RxList. (n.d.). *Haldol (Haloperidol): Side effects, interactions, warning, dosage & uses.* Retrieved from www.rxlist.com/haldol-drug.htm#side_effects_interactions

Soto, P. (2015). *Activated charcoal.* Poison Control, National Capital Poison Center. Retrieved from www.poison.org/articles/2015-mar/activated-charcoal

Swanson, A. (2015, April 30). A shocking number of mentally ill Americans end up in
     prison instead of treatment. *The Washington Post*. Retrieved from
     www.washingtonpost.com/news/wonk/wp/2015/04/30/a-shocking-number-of-
     mentally-il l-americans-end-up-in-prisons-instead-of-psychiatric-hospitals/
     ?noredirect=on&utm_term=.14cf96002bfd
Wikipedia. (n.d.). *Akathisia*. Retrieved from en.wikipedia.org/wiki/Akathisia
Wikipedia. (n.d.). *Extrapyramidal symptoms*. Retrieved from en.wikipedia.org/wiki/
     Extrapyramidalsymptoms

CHAPTER 8

State of Mind

Jelisa Lovette

What happened?
To that butterfly of a girl
Who wanted to meet everyone
Who loved everyone
Stones, diamonds, pearls
She was so full of life
So eager to win
No one could steal her smile
Sink or swim?
Alway swim
That's what she chose
Always friends never?
Gave everyone the benefit of doubt
That is until she had to learn to go without.
Without love
Without light
Without air
Death in near sight
She become weak
She lost her mind
She had no name
Seven years later
She's still trying to find something sane
Find her purpose
Dig her way out
But now she's locked up
Not allowed to shout
Can't speak her mind
None her concern
Death still near
Heart in ashes
Urn
She's slowly dying

© KONINKLIJKE BRILL NV, LEIDEN, 2020 | DOI: 10.1163/9789004441651_009

On the inside
She no longer has wings
She is a scorpion
Poisonous tail, sting
She's been reincarnated
Without the peace of death
This hurts worse
Because she can see
She has no innocence left

CHAPTER 9

The Call

Sandra Brown

> Awakenings require a woman to respond consciously, to accept the
> invitation to create herself anew, and to undertake the challenge, no mat-
> ter how frustrated or inadequate she may feel, thus each awakening call
> demands not only that it be heard, but that the woman finds the courage
> to trust and affirm the call, whenever it arises, wherever it takes her, and
> however much it challenges her way of being in the world.
>
> KATHLEEN NOBLE

∵

I remember the first time I heard what I believed was this call. I mistook it
for a random thought, being the precocious yet naive six year-old that I was, I
remember sensing how overwhelmed and frustrated my mother was, raising a
son and three daughters in the atmospheric anguish, anxiety, and abuse that
we came to internalize as home. Some of her fight and resolve had gone to
helping my brother battle leukemia and sickle-cell disease. Some of it went
to battling my father, who mistook our bodies for punching bags and faith-
fully devoted himself to Hodsco Construction Company and Anheuser-Busch.
What remained of my mother's fight and resolve went to working full-time odd
jobs, trusting my big sister to care for the rest of us until she got home.

We were all needy, tender-hearted children in our own way. My big sister
would rebel using laziness and the occasional lippiness that landed her in a
ton of trouble, but for her, negative attention was better than none, sometimes. She was my mother's first born and would by no means relinquish one
iota of love or attention, siblings be damned. Cuss, fuss, and fight as much as
my mother did, she acquiesced-maybe because my big sister needed her like
that-who knows? My brother never knew what wanting love and attention
was like. Momma wanted a boy and we all cradled him with it, rocked him in
it, protected him by it, and when he died, immortalized him through it. My
baby sister? Well, she's the baby, so like a million other mothers, my mother
catered to her baby girl who could never do wrong in her eyes and whenever

she considered the possibility, all it took was one of my sister's tantrums to justify her wrongs with excuses and rationalizations.

I needed my mother's love with an intensity too raw and deep for any words to remotely capture in meaning, but my child's brain chided me against burdening her any more than she already was. I'd see how happy bringing home good grades made her, and I lived to make her happy. The best scenario gave me four days out of the year to feel loved and doted upon. Those were report card days. More often than not, I lost two of those days to my mother's job, so I learned not to count on those days. I would hear her leave instructions with my big sister before going to work, so I would try to anticipate what she wanted and do it before she returned home. My mother was calling for reprieve, for relief, but I heard it as a call to me for happiness. If I could be the one child she didn't have to fuss at or worry about, I could make her happy. If I could make Momma happy, she would love me. So sometimes answering the call in my mind wasn't always about making her smile; most times it was about not upsetting her. Rather than throw tantrums or create problems at school (which is exactly what I did between fifth and eighth grade, but that's another story for another time), I would be quiet and stay out of the way.

To be fair, I don't think my mother asked me for this, but the louder I tried to answer the call, the more silent I became; at home, at school, inside my Self. I became what many middle children do: the invisible child. Apart from helping out at home or bringing home top grades, I learned to disappear. Sometimes it worked; I'd get lost in "The Adventures of Miss Switch" to escape the arguing and avoid being assigned as a substitute punching bag. I'd work weeks ahead at my homework as I'd hear Momma cussing my big sister out about her smart ass mouth and lazy ways. The more I listened for my mother's call, the harder it was to hear my own...

•••

Ignorance and silence have proven to be formidable teachers and guides on my journey. Being deaf to my own call left me open to answering calls not meant for me. My desire to unburden my mother at six turned into three conscious attempts at suicide by the time I was seventeen. In retrospect, I understand that I was not calling out for attention as some have said; neither was I crying out for help as others have believed. I'd internalized what I heard and was shown over the years: that I was a mistake. How can one discover who she is when nothing in her world affirms in her the truth that she deserves to be? That truth would introduce itself to me amid the methodical cacophony of medical staff desperately trying to revive me from ingesting all sixty-four of my mother's tranquilizers the night before. It came in a soft whisper; two words, in between sounds of flatlines, defibrillators, stomach pumps, and blinding lights.

In the midst of deafening chaos and the kind of sleep one never experiences on this side of eternity, I heard the words, "not yet." I can't say that I saw who said it, but what I heard for the first time was indeed my call, my invitation to discover who I really am, and to create my Self anew.

My decision to accept the call was instant. I was young, scared, and unsure, but it was okay to be those things, knowing that I deserved to be; whatever that entailed. My process, my journey, however, would take years, and in all honesty, is still ongoing. I left who I learned I wasn't, Lost who I thought I was, discovered who I was meant to be, and created my Self anew; all during different segments of my life's journey. Incarceration challenges my way of being on every level. What matters is that every day, sometimes every moment, I find the courage to affirm the call and trust the process: even here, especially here, and long after here.

CHAPTER 10

Pivotal Times

Angie Oakes

For the first seven years of my life I had a pretty good childhood. The house was nice, the yard was huge, there were plenty of kids to play with and my grandparents lived across the street from me. Life was good and I felt safe.

Grandpa never let my dad get too mad at me or my mom and brother.

Grandpa retired from his job when I was seven and he and grandma moved back to their home state of Tennessee. When they were gone, dad changed.

He started yelling and hitting all of us whenever he got angry.

One night when we were all having a good time together, dad and I were playing in the living room. We were trying to tickle each other and laughing. At some point, he claimed I pinched him. He picked me up and slammed me to the floor between his knees. He then put his hands around my neck and strangled me. The last thing I remember is struggling to breathe, terror and feeling myself pee before everything went black. I woke up on the bathroom floor with my mom hovering over me and crying, saying, "That's it, just breathe." She had done CPR to bring me back. My dad had literally choked the life out of me.

I realized right then that life would never be the same for me. Fear now became my new best friend. Fear of my dad and how easily he could take my life away.

• • •

Fifteen was a pivotal life for me. By this age, I was drinking daily to be drunk. I started taking LSD, pain medication, smoking, a lot of marijuana, and snorting cocaine.

Dad walked out on us and lived in another town. Mom would cry to me about him being gone and I needed to help with my brother. I had too much put on me, and I didn't know how to cope. I did the only thing I knew and that was to drink my stress away and to take drugs to numb my mind. I'd skip out of school with my friends to go party and hang out. I just didn't care about anything or anyone.

I was spinning out of control and I had no idea how to make it all stop. On one of these party days, I ended up with a couple of boys I didn't know. They weren't in school anymore. I don't remember how I ended up at his apartment,

© KONINKLIJKE BRILL NV, LEIDEN, 2020 | DOI: 10.1163/9789004441651_011

but he knew I'd been drinking. This 19 year-old boy forced me to have sex with him. I was so embarrassed and ashamed I never told anyone.

I just happened to go to school one day and my guidance counselor found me. He was concerned about why I'd missed so much school. I tried to blow him off, but he wouldn't have it. He got me to talk and I ended up telling him about my dad hitting my mom, my brother and me when he got around us. I didn't want to come to school with bruises, so I just skipped out. I had no idea he'd contact DCFS and file a report.

Someone from DCFS called my mom, but it was me who answered the phone. I played along and then freaked out. All I could do was run off. I had no idea what dad would do when he found out I'd told. I left my brother alone, and I ran. I had no money and no idea where to go. I had a friend no one knew about. I went to her house, made some calls and another friend had her boyfriend come get me. They hid me at some other peoples' house I didn't know.

I never really knew the danger I could be in. I slept fitfully, I was scared about my dad finding me.

Troy came and picked me and his friend Vicky up the next morning. We were going to a house out in Eureka. I only knew one way to get there, so we cut through the town I grew up in. I had cut my hair and changed the color of it so no one would recognize me. I heard my dad's motorcycle, I turned to see him behind us. I leaned up to Troy and told him to drive as fast as he could to the police station. I'd give him directions as we went.

We got to the station first and Troy went in to get me an officer. I saw Dad pull up and I hid in the car. Dad went into the station himself. I saw two officers go to Dad's motorcycle and remove a gun from the trunk. Another came to the car and asked me to step out and come into the station. I was escorted to a room where I waited alone.

My mom showed up and asked me where her daughter was. She didn't realize it was me with my hair different. She and I talked for a few minutes before a woman from the DCFS came in the room. This woman told me I had to go home with my parents. She believed my dad hadn't done anything to any of us. I remember her telling me I wouldn't know what abuse was if it hit me in the face. I told her she signed my death warrant, then reminded her he'd had a gun taken off him. She told me to shut up and go home.

I spent the next few years numb. I hated my life, I hated the people around me, and mostly, I hated myself. I nearly didn't care if I lived or died.

• • •

Just before I turned sixteen, I ended up living with my dad. As long as I lived with the devil, I could see the pain would come. For him to buy me a car all I had to do was get a job and keep passing grades. I found a job quick and I kept a C average. I never let my friends come to my house. I made a point to meet them wherever we want. I couldn't let dad see the type of people I hung out with nor could I let my friends see the man who caused me so much pain.

A job now gave me an excuse to be out of the house and make money to support my habits. I could buy pills, marijuana, alcohol, or whatever I wanted. The more Dad would hit me or belittle me, the higher I would try to get.

On my eighteenth birthday, Dad, a bunch of his friends, and I were drinking at the house. For a while it was actually fun. Then his best friend slid up next to me and said, "Your dad told me when you turned eighteen I could be your first."

I found no humor in it, and I told him flat out, "Sorry, but you're four years too late."

Then quickly got away. After everyone went home, Dad and I drank one last beer then he flipped out. He slapped me upside my head and started yelling about my being a ___ and the rules of his house. I just agreed to follow his rules so he'd stop and leave me alone. The next morning I told him, "If you ever put your hands on me again, I'd go to the cops. I'm of age now and I can press charges." He just blew me off.

The physical abuse stopped, but his verbal and psychological abuse got worse. It became a regular thing to hear how dumb and stupid I was. No one would ever want me and my favorite I was worthless. He has gone so far as to mess with my car to make it blow up. Lucky for me, I could work on my car and would know when something was wrong with it.

• • •

I met my ex-husband "C" that summer. He drank almost as much as I did. I guess you could say we started out as drinking buddies before we went out on our first date. He and I knew each other for about six months before I moved in with him and his family. I saw him as a means of escape from the hell I called home.

"C" and I had lived together for about a week when he pointed out to me that I was programmed to do what I was told to do. He'd tell me that if I wanted to do something to just do it, if I wanted to go somewhere to just go. I didn't need to wait to be told what to do or to ask permission. I never knew how much my dad controlled me. I quit school, I got married and I just did what I wanted. I drank, did drugs, and just had fun. I did have a job, I was hurt on the job about a year and a half prior. So my check is what kept us going.

• • •

At nineteen, I found out I was pregnant. I couldn't decide what I wanted to do. I never wanted to be married, nor did I ever see myself as a mother. I did stop drinking and doing drugs while I was pregnant. I was so unsure about what I was going to do and I didn't want to hurt the baby, so I cleaned up. At this point in life, I wasn't capable of taking care of myself, let alone another human being. The first time I feel the baby move I knew I had to figure out a way to care for this child and myself.

I was two months past my twentieth birthday when my daughter was born. The first time I held her in my arms I was overwhelmed. I knew I'd do anything to protect her from everything I'd ever been through. I didn't know how I was doing to do it, but I swore she'd have a better life than I had.

• • •

It wasn't long after I brought "N" home from the hospital that I was overcome with stress. I only knew one way to deal with stress, so I started drinking again. I was sucked back into my unhealthy family life with my dad, and I was trying to be a mom and a wife to a husband in jail.

I ended up doing just what I didn't want to do. I had my daughter around the monster I ran away from. I felt trapped and doomed, to repeat my history with my father with my daughter. The only way I could deal with my family was to drink, so I started drinking again.

I wasn't looking to get in trouble, but trouble found me. I ended up in jail with my brother. From there, I ended up in prison. My father was dead, so my daughter would never have to know the horrors of what I went through. My mom took over raising my daughter so I knew "N" would have the life I never got to know. I gave up my life so my daughter could have one.

CHAPTER 11

A Daughter's Sorrow

Sandra Brown

Doing time is nothing
Like serving life.
Time winds down,
Runs out,
Heals wounds,
Gives and takes,
And is at some point up.
Doing time
Comes with dates
That cease and desist
The monotonous
Misery of liberty On lockdown.
But serving life?
To that there's no end
When what binds you
Birthed you.

Tried before time,
Convicted at conception
And sentenced to life
From the womb.
I am forever
    Your living shame
    And dying dream;
    And tragic disaster.

Two score seven years,
I reach through timeless
Tears for you
And lose chunks of my soul.
Disempowered

© KONINKLIJKE BRILL NV, LEIDEN, 2020 | DOI: 10.1163/9789004441651_012

Disrespected,
Your words metastasize
Like Cancer,
Eating away
At my happiness
Because
No matter how happy
I can be
Want to be
Deserve to be,
Every fiber of my be-ing
Aches for you
To stop rejecting me
Like bad blood.

Betrayed at birth
I question my worth
Because of you.
Sometimes
I push love away
Because of you.
I fight life away
Because of you,
But I'm stuck
In self sabotage
Because of me.
Because I lack
The strength and sense
To let go.

"But you only get one,"
They say—
"Honor them
That thy days may be long."
My days be long all right—
Long with longing
To be yours
To be loved

To be mothered
To belong...

But I am sentenced
To a motherless life.

CHAPTER 12

Talking It out from the Inside

Cara Quiett

If you ever find yourself incarcerated and feeling suicidal, whatever you do, keep it to yourself. That was my motto. It did not take long for me to figure out how suicidal offenders are treated in the system.

Not that I expected a room of soft kittens and aromatherapy with Michael Buble crooning in the background. No, of course the state could not facilitate that. But I had figured out that things could get worse for me if I expressed too much grief. That could have been in the form of; sad words, chronic sobbing, and lack of appetite.

The answer for that was frigid solitude. The uniform for the ones at risk of themselves was a forever-pissy, velcro quilt. It was as itchy as steel wool and about as comforting as snuggling up to a burning garbage bag of random human hair. Shoes, gone. Toilet, a person could drown themselves. Suicide watch was a cell with a hole in the floor and an overpaid babysitter watching every boring hour. As appealing as all that seemed, I decided to clutch dearly to the small accommodations that I had left. Not so much for myself, but for my only son.

The rockstar of my heart, it was bad enough I had to be away. I could not bear the thought of causing his young mind to worry more than necessary.

Kenny was ten and old enough to know the things that kids easily find out. Between other people, the news and the internet. There was just no point in lying to him. Before I was cuffed and hauled off, I knelt in front of him and confessed. I looked him in the eyes and told him because I wanted him to hear the truth from me first as opposed to a lie from someone else.

Right before me, a storm rolled in the blue pigment of his eyes. Instantly, his face grew longer and older and it was like we simultaneously came to the harsh realization that things would never be the same.

There I was in the county jail waiting to be sequestered far away to fulfill my legal obligation. In the meantime, at least my son was close. He was brought to visit me regularly. A luxury I knew I was going to have to learn to live without the up and coming months.

In the movies and shows, inmates visit with civilians through a single sheer pain of plexiglass, and a black phone. Due to the advancement of shoddy technology, my experience was much more complicated.

© KONINKLIJKE BRILL NV, LEIDEN, 2020 | DOI: 10.1163/9789004441651_013

My visitors were in a different building being video recorded in real time while I was in a booth on my temporary housing pod. The process was better than nothing but it hardly ever worked properly. The sound was usually off on one side or the other. The timer had a habit of cutting off minutes before my visits were over. Leaving out the chance to say those last precious farewells and I love you's.

But... it was better than nothing.

One day, after being summoned from my cell via intercom, I walked with a pep in my step to receive a visit from my son. I entered the dookie brown booth and sat on the silver stool anxiously waiting. The Jeopardy theme song played over in my head, do-do-do-do-do-do-doooo.

At last! After digging under my nails for what felt like hours, his familiar image finally sprung the screen to life.

"Hi Mom!" he chided with a massive grin, just for me.

"Hi sweetie," I replied as my heart was choking me to leap out of its comfy notch through my windpipe, past my mouth, into the phone, coating the wires like electricity to bold free to hug him to pieces.

"What is going on?" I asked, trying to sound cheerful.

"Oh, not much, just here to see you."

"Hey Mom, when are you coming home?"

The fragile but heavy question he had been asking that I did not have the answer to.

At that point, the State's Attorney had offered me ten years at eighty-five percent, but the maximum amount of time I could serve was fourteen years. Now, I am not complaining that my offer was unfair. I just did not know how to explain this to my son. After all, ten years was his lifetime. All I could say was, "It is not going to be for a while, I do not know how long this will take."

Kenny hung his head while he processed my response. Quickly, he rebounded, snapping his head back up like a spring-loaded Pez dispenser. Clearly pissed and hurt he said, "What does that mean? That is all you ever say! Is a long time a week, two weeks?"

In my mind I was thinking, more like years, son. I decided that it was time to start easing him into my long, inevitable stay away.

"Well," gulp, "no matter how long I am gone, just remember that I am always with you. You can talk to me with your heart, and there will be your answer." I have never fought back tears so hard. I was drowning in a brick desert.

After a deep breath, I continued, "Son, now try not to get too upset. I can not say for sure what will happen, but the State's Attorney has offered me ten years."

"Ten years!" he exclaimed.

"Calm down, try not to worry. I am not taking their offer, but they could give me as much as fourteen years."

"Fourteen years!" he shouted, even louder.

"I know, I know that it sounds like a long time for someone your age, but try to believe me when I say that it will go by fast, and I am doing everything I can to get home to you. But I will be lucky to be out before you graduate high school. You know I would come home right now if I could but that is just not possible."

The conversation flatlined as a piercing silence engulfed the moments that followed. "I am sorry honey, try to tell me. How do you feel?" His lips did this thing where they would pucker sourly to the right corner of his mouth when he was nervous. Coaxing, I said, "We have to try and talk about it. It's not healthy to bury your feelings forever. You have to let them out to be free."

"I don't want to tell you, Mom," he said gazing at me through defeated eyes.

"Oh, come on, I can tell by your twisted-up mouth that you have a lot to say."

"I don't want to worry you Mom!"

"Honey, that is what I am here for. I cannot do much for you right now, but I can listen, and no matter what you ever told me, I would never ever love you any less." Kenny relaxed his lips and squinted, as if he was trying to see the unseeable.

"It's like... something is always missing now. Like someone chopped off my arm. While I was building a snowman, it was harder because it felt like part of me was gone."

Boom, mushroom cloud where my heart resided. Well, at least I got him to share but this was too much. Especially since I know full well that I was the one to cause him all that pain.

Just another straw in the sticky victim web my actions had woven. A web that suffocated my soul, drained it of its dreams, and left nothing but a dusty carcass. His words were profound but I was proud of him for having the courage to speak. To reveal things that hurt in such an eloquent way for a child his age, is a task that even intelligent adults struggle to do.

The drowning sensation returned as I fought back more tears. Air, fuck, I need air.

"Thank you for sharing honey, it is good to talk about how you feel. I am sorry I hurt you but even though you cannot see me, I am always with you." It was a cliché thing to say, I knew, but what else could I say?

Both of us on the verge of an emotional melt down and I could not help but notice the clock in the bottom left corner. Red numbers telling me how much time I have left of my visit. Changing the subject, I switched gears, downshifting before we crashed.

"How is Peyton?" I asked about our dog. "He is good. He is still getting in the trash, though." "Are you taking him out every day?" I asked.

"Of course," he said.

"Give him lots of snuggles and kisses from me, but be careful about the trash. You know he will eat anything."

Kenny giggled. "I know."

It has been six years since those video visits. I am still parenting from over a hundred and thirty miles away with weekly phone calls and a couple of visits a year. I have tried my best to balance our conversations between fun-loving and parental. Sometimes it is a corny mom joke and other times I have had to get on his case about homework. Through it all, he still trusts me. He shared his fears of his father's heroin addiction, when he lost his virginity, his own recreational marijuana use, and girl troubles.

A lot can change in a boy between the ages of ten to seventeen. I believe the changes I saw were more startling and abrupt because they were witnessed in leaps and bounds. Plus, I was not physically there to have much control. Lately, Kenny's voice is full of base and mostly hope. We are both excited that I will be returning soon. Don't get me wrong, he is still a teenager and can say some straight up mean, reckless stuff. The kind of stuff that makes me call my mom and apologize to her for spitting venomous words over twenty years ago. I call him on his back talk, we recover and move forward. The way I imagine most normal parents to teenagers do.

Prison has definitely brought more value to my conversations. Those little thirty-minute talks have, at times, been all I have had to look forward to. I try to be mindful of every prayer, promise, and statement. With so many victims in my wake, I have made it my new business, not to offend. Even if it is just with cheap words, talk that could have placed me in a straightjacket years ago, instead of loosely holding bonds together.

CHAPTER 13

Mother-Less Child

Jelisa Lovette

Sometimes I feel like a motherless child,
Running wild, confused on which direction
I am to go in life
Stuck in a cold, dark
Place, nowhere to run, no-one to talk to and
Constantly paying every price
Accepting all actions for my mistakes but knowing every
Consequence I get isn't right So I must fight!

Sometimes I feel like a motherless child
A long way from home but dats because I am,
Stuck in dis place, dis prison where they try to
Force my everyday purpose to serve da Man.
But I know my big day is coming soon because
I am following God's plan
And wen dat day comes
That's wen the startn' chapter of my new life
Will begin

Sometimes I feel like a mother-less child
Growing up my mom was present but
In her own world
Lookn' after my baby brothers
Substituting for our mother
Whenever she felt da need to wanna party
We had everything we wanted including a mother's
Unconditional love, tsss yea hardly
But as kids all we care about are toys, candy, birthday parties

Sometimes I feel like a mother-less child,
Braking all da rules, with da wrong tools, caused
Me to drop outta high school
While everyone else saw the world as black and white,

I saw green and red
There was money to be made and sometimes da
Price to pay was blood that had to be shed
All because of a mother-less child,
Started smokin' weed, popn pills, got addicted to black and
Mild—shit I went crazy fuck wild

But being a motherless child, it wasn't all bad
I was forced into maturity, forced to raise my brothers
to be the best dads
Speaking of dads I was blessed with 2,
But down da path in my life, no-one not
Even my mother really knew what I went
Thru

I lost both of my dads, one to da
Grave and the other to the Illinois department
Of corrections- never really knowing
Who to give my love and affections, never
Knowing how to deal with neglection, so I
Give my love to all the wrong ones

Just like dat caged bird I must confess

That I once was a child who knows what it
Feels like to be motherless.
A mother-less child...

CHAPTER 14

Not Waving, Not Drowning

Sandra Brown

I am flailing in the heart of the Bermuda triangle, hypothermic and weak from persistently cold and violent waves. Survival instincts force me to keep my nose above water, but the constant stinging and coughing from these bouts of drowning, this constant asphyxiation, make my lungs beg to explode and be done with it all. But I am a Capricorn, half goat and half fish; too stubborn to die and too flexible to break. I hold in my hands yet another rejection letter, worded ever so beautifully from another college about another doctoral program. "The issue is not that you are an incarcerated student. Your Statement of Purpose raises issues so blatantly ignored in today's global community. You bring a perspective so vitally unique to any doctoral program in which you choose to pursue. Your lack of computer/internet access, however, poses a debilitating barrier to your educational opportunities. You are an exceptionally bright candidate, and we hope that you will have access to technology soon so that we may assist you in your academic endeavors."

When I started trying to swim upstream, I anticipated challenges, I expected a struggle. Nothing worth having ever came without a fight for it. I fought for love, respect, food, first-place, scholarships—FOR MY LIFE. Life makes me fight for everything that I am fortunate enough to have. "Indeed a glaring gap exists in correctional education," the letter says; as did the letter before that and the letter before that... AND the letter before that. Tell me something I don't know already-I'm the one who reminded THEM! Who is willing to step up to the plate and help close the gap? That's what I want to know. I don't want a hand-out and have never asked for one. What I've worked my ass off for, however, is a way out.

I've gone hungry saving every nickel and dime that I could, written countless scholarship essays, and studied infinitely harder than I ever would have in the free community to demonstrate that I am not "just another stupid inmate." I feel myself gasping for hope, yet floundering in this torrential sea of defeat. How did I get here and why can't I ever seem to find dry land?

I look at the beautifully worded letters, all of them ending with some well-intentioned but superficial wish of good luck with my pursuits and "Not Waving but Drowning" flashes across my mind. Did Stevie Smith write that? How is it possible to know what it's like to drown in dry air? To drown in dryness... barrenness?

The labels, the powerlessness shackle themselves around my ankles, and I feel the weight, pulling me down to my death with the force of a two-ton anchor. I gasp violently, inhaling my hopes and clinging to my dreams, which now serve as lifesavers.

Inhale, I wanna be a teacher when I grow up; coughing, you're an inmate now-you'll never teach in a classroom again.

Gasp, hold-fast-to-dreams-for-when-dreams-die-life-is-a-broken-winged-bird-that-cannot-fly.

I'm tired of fighting. I'm tired of swimming in the middle of nowhere. Bre athe! Inmate? Doctor? Prisoner? Professor? Sink? Or Swim? GASP! You know you were built for this... so get swimming!

CHAPTER 15

Isaac

Claire Prendergast

I think Isaac is one of my soul mates. He's always understood me in a way that not many other people do. You know people often say they understand how you feel, but you can kinda tell that they really don't? I don't get that with Isaac. I feel like he really truly understands me. In some ways, that's kinda sad, because it means we both know what depression feels like in the same way, and I wouldn't wish that feeling on anyone. But it's nice to have someone with whom I can connect with so deeply about that.

He's been writing a lot lately. When we were kids in high school, he used to write a lot of poetry all the time, probably three new poems every day, but he hadn't been writing much in the last five years. I think art is important. I told Isaac, "If I am not creating something, I am destroying myself."

I think that humans have an innate need to create things. I think people who are profoundly unhappy need to re-channel that energy into creation, because energy must be spent. I don't want to spend my energy on self-destruction. I want to spend it on creation. When I said that to Isaac, he said, "I've never thought of it that way." I hope that means he'll take that concept into consideration. He's been sending me a lot of his poems and photography, and I just hope he keeps creating, because I don't want to see him destroy himself again.

He doesn't know how smart he is. He's an intellectual. I don't think he thinks of himself as an intellectual, but everyone else thinks of him that way. When I went to college, and Isaac stayed behind in our hometown, every time I came home to visit, I would try to convince him to come join me at school. I promised him he would fit in on my campus, and I meant it. I can even see him sitting in undergraduate classes, bored because the material is beneath him. Not that he's pretentious. He's extremely unpretentious, and, when he does exhibit some kind of pretension, he's extremely self-aware and has a sense of humor about it. He's always quoting famous authors. I wonder if he's afraid to take any credit for his own thoughts so attributes them to people greater than him. People like Oscar Wilde. I think Isaac is great like Oscar Wilde.

He's been my best friend for fifteen years. We met freshman year of high school, at a football game, behind the bleachers where the burnouts and stoners made out or smoked cigarettes. Back then, we took a lot of the same

© KONINKLIJKE BRILL NV, LEIDEN, 2020 | DOI: 10.1163/9789004441651_016

classes together. As many as we could. In our history of religion course, we did a project together on Satanism. We thought we had picked an edgy subject that would scare our parents and ended up learning that the religion is more of a parody than anything else. In physical education, we were the two who were always picked last. But during the ping-pong unit we were the best pair in the class, earning the respect of the jocks we beat. I could remember the combination to his locker but not mine. He loaned me his copy of The Perks of Being a Wallflower and burned me a copy of Say Anything's first studio album. He watched my favorite anime when I loaned him the DVD, even though anime wasn't something he was particularly interested in.

Sometimes Isaac would wear eyeliner, like the lead singer of My Chemical Romance or one of his other favorite bands. And because it looked good on him. One time a dean decided that boys shouldn't wear eyeliner at our high school, and Isaac was told to wash his face. Over the course of the following week, a campaign was started by our peers in his defense, and, by the end of the week, almost every boy at school was wearing thick black makeup around their eyes. Of course, none of them applied it as well as Isaac had.

We auditioned for plays together, and he started as an extra and ended up with small roles by junior year, while I never did well at auditions and always ended up on the stage crew. Our senior year, Isaac directed a theatre production of Shirley Jackson's The Lottery, a horror story that has always been a favorite of mine. I didn't bother to try out for that one. I wanted to be in the audience for once. I hired him to play Johnny in my shot-for-shot remake of the opening scene of Night of the Living Dead for my film class. His acting was so in line with the original that the girl I had gotten to play Barbara couldn't stop laughing. We would go together to see our friends play in their shitty punk rock bands at local shows and he would bring his camera.

We hated high school. We only managed to have any good memories of that time because we had found each other and formed a merry band of misfits around us. Recently, we discussed whether or not to go to our ten-year reunion. I said I would rather die, but he said we could go if we could come up with a really good lie, like in the movie Romy and Michele's High School Reunion, where the titular characters falsely tell their old classmates that they had invented post-its.

After high school was over, Isaac's friendship was one of the only ones that I kept. His house was the place to be when we were in our early twenties. Well, his parent's house was the place to be. We used to hang out in a shed in their backyard. I mean, it wasn't really a shed—it was like a motorcycle garage that we had converted into our clubhouse. We called it "The Shed." It was a place where anyone and everyone was welcome, and Isaac was the perfect host for the perpetual party of our early twenties. I think a lot of us who hung out there weren't there for the party, though. We were there for Isaac.

The Shed was cool back then. There were two couches that took up the longer walls. There were a couple of chairs and a mini fridge that was almost always stocked with beer and liquor, and Isaac always had marijuana to share. There was a table in the center of the room big enough for a pizza box and a board game. Isaac had brought out his speaker system and anyone was welcome to plug their iPods into it. We could listen to anything, and everyone's music was worth hearing at least once, even if indie rock was our preference. Every now and then we would put on show tunes. Nobody besides Isaac and I enjoyed that, especially because he and I couldn't help but sing along.

He would ask me for posters from the movie theater, where I worked, to put up on the walls in what little spaces weren't already covered in art. He asked to buy art from me. Isaac was the first person to ever buy artwork from me, and he displayed it proudly in The Shed, where all of our friends could see it. We did everything there. We watched movies, shared meals, and sometimes someone would sleep in there. Whoever's parents were fed up with their shit could always stay the night in The Shed.

We would talk about everything. Life. Love. Art. Philosophy and religion. Isaac had an interest in astrology and ancient religions that he could talk about for hours. He kept a book about astrology that had a page for every day of the year that told you who you are based on when you were born and his friends and their friends wrote their names in it. There were probably over a hundred names in that book.

Eventually, Isaac and a couple of the guys we would hang out with rented a house together and that became the new place to party. But, for a while anyway, The Shed was really the coolest place to be.

I don't know exactly when it is that partying becomes a problem but, for me, it was four years ago, around age 24. I needed to make a change in my life, so I left. I went to college. For a while, I would see Isaac every time I came home to visit, doing the same things we did in The Shed. And then, for a while, I didn't hear from him at all.

• • •

I don't remember exactly how the conversation went. I remember how I felt. How I feel now. Afraid. Heartbroken.

"Have you told your family yet?"

"I literally just hung up the phone with the doctor and called you."

I'm glad he called me. I was the right person to call. Not only because I consider him my best friend, but because I'm good at dealing with all kinds of big emotional crises.

"Did the doctor say AIDS or HIV?"

"You know what, I don't even know, I think he said AIDS? I am not sure honestly."

"Holy shit. Call the doctor back and ask. You want to know if it's HIV or like Full Blown AIDS? Right?"

"Oh my god, right? I'll call him back, I just, I had to call you."

It is an honor to be the person he called.

"They expect you'll call back. My dad told me that back in 1984, he had to get his cancer diagnosis told to him three times before it sunk in. They expect you'll call them back with these sorts of things."

"Right? Okay. I'll call back when we hang up."

"You don't sound upset? You must be in shock. I mean this isn't happening to me and I am in shock."

But I'm pretty sure the only reason I held it together during this particular emotional crisis is because I was in shock. I wasn't entirely shocked, but I was certainly in shock.

"Are you supposed to call anyone you've been with?"

"The doctor didn't tell me to but like yes right? But like, with NA, I'm not supposed to talk to anyone I used to use with either."

"Did you get this from sex or drug use? I'm sorry. I just-"

"No, I mean, I don't know? And it would be the same guys either way. I think."

• • •

The first thing I did after I got that phone call from Isaac was call my dad. It was hard to say it. It was hard to get the words to come out of my mouth. When they did, my voice felt small, like I was a little girl again.

"Dad. Isaac has AIDS." That is when the shock began to wear away and tears began to cloud my sight.

Immediately, my dad replied, without any hesitation, "He's in more danger of dying of an overdose than AIDS right now." I didn't know if that was true. I thought that AIDS was a death sentence. All the movies about AIDS are set in the 80s, and back then it was a death sentence. That's the only framework that I had to work with to imagine the possible outcomes for my friend.

"He just got out of rehab, you know how this goes," my dad said. "You've had other friends go through this. You know that this is the time when he's most likely to overdose." I really cried hard that night.

I have had other friends who got mixed up in drugs, but none of them were Isaac.

• • •

About a week after I found out that Isaac has HIV, the TED Talk "Our Treatment of HIV Has Advanced, So Why Hasn't The Stigma?" popped into my YouTube feed one morning. An attractive and stylish young man with a beard appeared on my computer screen talking about his diagnosis. It felt serendipitous; this particular video was uploaded to YouTube so soon after HIV entered my life through my best friend. TED Talks are a lot like these autoethnographies we write in the critical storytelling class I am taking for the second time, the kind of autoethnography I am writing right now. We tell personal stories that intersect with larger cultural issues.

Arik Hartmann told his story to an audience at TEDxVermilionStreet in 2016, about getting diagnosed with HIV and making his status known on Grindr, the dating app exclusively for gay men. The same app where, I am sure without being told, Isaac met the man who gave him this disease, whoever he is. Grindr is not meant to be an educational tool, it's an app for gay men to find other gay men to hook up with, but Hartmann used it to connect with gay men to educate his community about HIV.

I felt comforted by Mr. Hartmann's TED Talk. He looks healthy. He doesn't look like those photographs of gay men in the 1980s and 90s in New York and that's the point of his TED Talk. He begins by showing his audience the famous 1990 Life magazine photograph of David Kirby with his family as he is dying from AIDS. It's a strong juxtaposition, this comparison of then and now. He asks his audience if they know that "with treatment, those with HIV not only fend off AIDS completely, but they live full and normal lives?" There is a show of hands and laughter as he says "Ya'll are educated." He asks his audience if they know that with treatment, HIV can become undetectable and virtually uninfectious. Less hands are raised. He then asks them if they know "of the pre- and post-exposure treatments that are available that reduce the risk of transmission by over 90 percent?" No. I didn't know that. I didn't know any of that. All the stories I know are from the 80s and 90s. I'm grateful to Mr. Hartmann for telling his story and for sharing his HIV positive status with other young gay men who are afraid and alone.

• • •

It took me a while to call my mom about it. I didn't want to tell her because of the stories she had told me about Walter. When I was a baby, my parent's friend Walter was dying of AIDS. The story I hear most often from mom is about a party, where everyone is passing around the baby, me. And it's 1990, so nobody really knows what's going on, and they're scared, so they're keeping me away from Walter. Walter died not long after, and I wish he could have held me. We now know that a man with AIDS can hold a baby, and he won't somehow transfer his disease.

When I finally told my mom and she cried with me, she said, "I have to be honest, with his promiscuity and drug use I always worried about this." I wish we were all more surprised. The saddest part of Isaac getting HIV, in my perspective, is that nobody is really all that surprised.

Mom said nobody was really surprised about Walter either: "He had been hanging out in the bathhouses in New York." And it was the late 80s. I'm angry at Isaac for his promiscuity at this moment, but I don't exactly blame him. Of course gay men are more promiscuous. There's no women around to say 'no,' right? The old joke goes that gay men have sex as often as straight men want to. I think there's some truth in that.

As we discussed the scary possibilities of the future, we also contemplated the past. My mom said, "I remember when I first met Isaac. I thought he was just the cutest kid, and I was honestly disappointed that you said he was gay, because he would have been so cute with you." She's not wrong, but I sort of am glad that Isaac is gay, because there has never been any worry with him the way there can be with other friendships I have had with men. It's nice to have a male friend with whom you never have to worry about falling in love or having sexual tension. Not that I'm not sort of in love with Isaac. I think that Isaac is very easy to fall in love with and just about everyone who meets him is in love with him. At least a little bit. The majority of Isaac's ex-boyfriends were 'straight' men who saw Isaac as the only exception to their heterosexuality. I personally believe these men to be bisexual and likely uncomfortable with their attraction to men. I think it says a lot about who Isaac is that men who are uncomfortable even admitting to their bisexuality can admit to being in love with him. Men have changed their entire lives and outed themselves just to spend a little bit of time with Isaac.

• • •

For a couple months, things seemed to move along smoothly. After finishing his inpatient drug rehab, Isaac moved to Texas to stay with his grandparents. While there, he went to Narcotics Anonymous meetings daily and called me every few days. He started talking about college. He found a free clinic where he could get medications to make his HIV undetectable. The doctors told him that with just one pill a day he could his blood-work could look like that of someone without HIV in only six months. We talked about a lot of things. I mostly listened. I don't think he went into full detail about anything that we talked about. I read every poem he shared with me. Poems about heavy stones that represent regret and dying stars that represent all the things he could have been. He talked about going back to school.

One of the last things he said to me in a phone call from Texas was that he wasn't sure about the twelve-step program. He said he thought he'd do better in counseling, with "some kind of therapist or something." He said he could get counseling from the HIV clinic. I think Isaac has needed therapy since we were kids. Sometimes I think that if I hadn't gotten therapy, I could have ended up where he is now. On drugs instead of in college. That profound sadness that has connected us led us both down some bad paths in life, but I got help and I got out and I left and went to college before things went too far. I never did any drugs besides pot. Isaac has done every drug.

• • •

Isaac was supposed to visit me over spring break, but I didn't hear from him. He was supposed to come back to Illinois for a surgery that he needed. I didn't think Illinois was a good idea, but he wanted to see his usual doctor. I was afraid he would visit some old friends that he shouldn't visit if he came back, but I did want him to visit me. I miss him. I have missed him for a very long time.

I messaged him online on Sunday. "You in Illinois? How you do, bro?"

The chat program indicated that he had read my message but he did not reply.

I messaged him on Monday. "I hope you doin good I miss you."

The chat program indicated that he had read my message but he did not reply.

I messaged him on Tuesday as I began to lose hope that I would see him.

"DID YOU GET YOUR SURGICAL PROCEDURE DONE? I AM CONCERNED FOR YOU, MY FRIEND."

The chat program indicated that he had read my message but he did not reply.

On Wednesday I sent him a meme. I guess I thought that maybe if he wasn't interested in words I could still make him laugh. The chat program indicated that he had seen the meme but he did not reply. Not even a laughing face emoji or a simple "LOL."

On Thursday I was out of patience. I had spent the week of spring break moving from fear and anxiety to anger. I decided this was the last time I would say anything without a response. I decided to tell him exactly what I was thinking. Each day that passed without a response from him made me lose more hope and by Thursday I was sure that he had relapsed.

"HEY ASSHOLE, IF I DON'T HEAR BACK FROM YOU I AM GOING TO ASSUME YOU ARE ON THE DRUGS OR DEAD OR BOTH SO DON'T BE AN ASSHOLE. I LOVE YOU AND I MISS YOU."

I thought back to what my dad said the night I found out that Isaac has HIV. That Isaac is in more danger of dying of an overdose. I know what Isaac was using, and I know he was using it with the men he slept with. So I started to do some research. I don't know what kind of website I expected tweaker.org to be, but it's a website for gay men to learn about methamphetamine. I had already learned from Isaac that there is a subculture of gay men who will do meth together. What I learn from this website is that they will use meth together and fuck for days. Literally days. Hours and days of continuous non-stop sex. I'm horrified to read that. I'm horrified to type it. I don't want to think about it. Isaac had sort of told me that this is what he had been doing, but he didn't say it so directly.

On tweaker.org I learn a lot of things that I wish I hadn't. I read a lot of things that make me feel sick. I thought that doing research and writing this would help me feel better, to understand what is happening to my friend. It just makes me more anxious, more afraid that he is going to die. A page on the site labeled "Crystal and HIV" says "For HIV positive guys who use crystal, the demanding lifestyle of the user can lead to a lapse in taking HIV medications."

That is when I scrolled to the bottom of the page and learned that the site was put together by the San Francisco AIDS Foundation. I know now for sure, if AIDS kills my friend, it will be because of his drug use. A diagnosis of HIV in 2018 is not a death sentence. It's Isaac's lifestyle that could kill him.

Gay men are not who I imagine when I imagine a meth addict. I imagine that skinny guy from Breaking Bad with sunken eyes and scars on his face. I don't imagine someone like Isaac. None of the characters who used meth on Breaking Bad were attractive and intelligent young gay men.

According to an article titled "The Changing Face Of Meth" from the *Huffington Post*, "In gay circles, the drug is often used as a 'party' drug whereby users partake in the drug's euphoric properties to sometimes engage in prolonged sexual experiences, including risky behaviors like unprotected and group sex. Researchers suspect this behavior has facilitated the spread of HIV." I have been offered a lot of drugs in my life. I've been offered cocaine, acid, ecstasy, but never methamphetamine. This article says that, in the gay community, "meth is so pervasive that 71% of gay and bisexual men who were surveyed said they have been asked to try crystal meth." The article also says that dating apps like Grindr may have made it easier to buy and sell this drug.

And I found a dozen other articles that say the same things. On New-NowNext, an LGBT news site, the headline is "How Meth Is Devastating The World's Gayest Cities." It says that, according to the CDC, in New York City the use of methamphetamine has more than doubled among gay and bisexual men since 2011. They call it "Party and Play," The party is the drug use, the play is the sex that follows. Gay men who are interested in it put "PnP" on their Grindr profiles. They also call it "chemsex." I wonder what Isaac's profile on Grindr says now. I wonder if he just looked for "PnP" on other men's profiles or if he listed it on his. I hope that he's deleted the app from his phone but I know, because I am not hearing back from him, it's not likely.

This is not what I had imagined for my friend when we were kids or as he grew into a beautiful and brilliant young man, who could make anyone fall in love with him. I had imagined him being a published author, a Broadway play director, a professor of philosophy, and the founder of a brand new religion.

It was three days after I called him an asshole when I finally got a response. "Sorry I've been a shitty friend. Just fell back into everything and ended up fucking up harder than before. I'm alive hopefully checking myself back into rehab tomorrow."

I told him he's my best friend. I told him I love him. I told him to call me. He hasn't.

References

Hartmann, A. (n.d.). *Our treatment of HIV has advanced, why hasn't the stigma changed?* Retrieved from https://www.ted.com/talks/arik_hartmann_our_treatment_of_hiv_has_advanced_why_hasn_ _the_stigma_changed

San Francisco AIDS Foundation. (n.d.). Crystal and HIV. *Tweaker.* Retrieved from http://tweaker.org/

Shucart, B. (2017, June 14). How meth is devastating the world's gayest cities. *NewNowNext.* Retrieved from https://www.newnownext.com/meth-gay-men/06/2017/

Stanger, E., & Porter, R. L. (2017, December 1). The changing face of meth. *HuffPost.* Retrieved from https://www.huffingtonpost.com/entry/the-changing-face-of-meth_us_58b849d9e4b051155b 4f8c7d

CHAPTER 16

Prison

Angie Oaks

When I first stepped into Dwight Correctional Center here in Illinois, I was 22 years old. I found myself to be nervous yet curious at the same time. I had no idea what to expect from the guards or the inmates. All I knew about prison was what I had seen in movies and the few male friends I had who had been locked up before.

I spent the first week in what's called "intake status." Meaning I had to stay in my room until my medical tests came back declaring me healthy and clear of communicable diseases and for my security level and escape risk to be determined. I spent three days with an older woman as my roommate. She had been here before and she told me I'd be fine.

"Honey, just do what you need to do. Follow the c.o.'s orders, pick good people to hang out with, and you'll do fine. It'll be over before you know it."

I never told her I had 28 years left to do. Even now, 23 years later, I can still hear her words in my head. If only I could tell her she was right.

While in intake I requested to be assigned to the drug and alcohol rehab unit. I needed to understand my addictions and how to cope as a sober person. I did learn that I could cope with stress without pills or alcohol. It was not easy and I had a long road to walk. I learned how to be accountable for my choices and actions. These were lessons I needed to learn.

I also learned how to teach people. My counselor thought it would be good for me to run the units orientation into the program. I didn't like to talk in groups, so this was her idea to get me to talk.

I left the program after 90 days and lived in general population. I was maximum security still, so I had to live in a max unit. We had to do our laundry by hand, be locked in our rooms at 9pm, and I couldn't buy microwavable foods. I worked in the kitchen until I was put in school. I passed my GED test when I was in the County Jail, so I signed up for college when I left intake.

I found out that I really loved being in school. I was in Culinary Arts full-time and three academic classes part time. I had the opportunity to take all the college vocational and academic classes I wanted and I did just that. I spent the next 10 years in school making the best out of a bad situation. I just liked each day in my community called Dwight as a student, an employee at my different job assignments, a volunteer as a reading and math teacher, a friend and roommate.

After that much time in one place, I was ready for a change. I needed a new start, so I requested transfer to Lincoln Correctional Center. The whole place was different. Now instead of one roommate, I had 19. The showers were open like the ones back in high school, along with the bathroom. I was used to being around other inmates like myself who had lengthy sentences. Now I was around more inmates who had short sentences.

I spent more time at this prison just being and trying to focus on myself. I did so much for other people when I was at Dwight that I didn't do things for myself. I still needed to fix myself. I became involved in self-help groups trying to help heal my deep wounds. I needed to console my injured and scared inner child, to hold the hand of my addicted self and to let her know everything would be okay sober, and to let my imperfect adult know it was perfectly okay to be imperfect.

Chaos happened when Illinois decided to push all the women into two prisons. I spent three years in Logan Correctional Center. This was the worst of all my time in prison. The fights were bad now. Women were cutting each other with razors, broken mirrors, throwing boiling water at each other. The staff had no way of controlling the hoard.

When Dwight and Lincoln were combined at Logan, the rules were all suspended due to the "trauma of transfer," and control has never again regained at Logan. I believed this was the environment I would finish my time in.

I was working in the lower library at Logan one day, when my boss told me I was being transferred to Decatur Correctional Center. This was something I never saw coming. Decatur is a minimum security prison, and I had been told my charges (since they are violent) would keep me from going. Part of me was happy to be getting away from the conditions of Logan, and part of me was sad to be leaving all the people I love and care about.

After a couple of months here at Decatur, I realized there was something I needed to do. I finally came to see that I needed to get some help from mental health. My anxiety was out of control; I couldn't sleep; my mood was all up and down; I even felt aggressive at times. I started seeing a therapist and talking about my life before and during prison. I talked with a psychiatrist and we decided to try a low dose of meds for PTSD, anxiety, and depression. Being on the medication has helped me rebuild old relationships, make my friendships better and to understand myself.

Prison is seen as a dark, violent place void of love and enjoyment. It's not always like that. I never wanted to be in prison, yet I found myself here. I made the best out of my situation. I have met some of the most amazing people in my 25 years. People that I would have never met had we not all been in this mess together. I have formed bonds and friendships that will not cease when I walk out of these gates. I have managed to make my negative experience and turn it into the most positive experience I could.

Prison saved me from killing myself slowly with my addictions and unchecked mental health issues. For that I am grateful. I'm ready now for the next transition in my life and that is my release from prison.

CHAPTER 17

Love Find Me

Jelisa Lovette

Withdrawn into my own world
Tired and no longer chasing after
The mirage of love.
But hoping that one day, a true love will find
Me here, layin' underneath all of this pain and grief.
Still alive. But unable to sleep. So, I stay
Awake, daydreaming of a day that doesn't
seem to be getting any closer to my reality.
So far away from my reality.
I'm walking barefoot over top of broken
Promises and shattered dreams. Open wounds
Profusely bleeding out hope, until I'm hopeless
The hope dat love exists fades away with the
Thought like mist, my thoughts of love have kept
Me in obscurity, lost, but still hoping that
One day love finds me, a love that will truly
Last an eternity.

© KONINKLIJKE BRILL NV, LEIDEN, 2020 | DOI: 10.1163/9789004441651_018

CHAPTER 18

Little Girl Lost

Angie Oakes

Little girl lost…
She knows not what to do,
Who to trust or where to go.
Her life is a struggle to breathe.
She never feels safe.
Always looking over her shoulder.
Can never let her face tell how she really feels.
Must be a fake to others.
A wearer of many masks.
Never knowing which one is real.
Cowering bruises and split lips.
Can't tell or ask for help.
Heart full of pain.
Must make it step.
Tears never helped or saved anyone.
Turns off her feelings.
Puts her heart on cement.
Better to feel nothing.
Swallowing, snorting, and smoking.
The world is blurry, yet she floats.
Left hit, left hit, right hit, lights out.
Swallow, snort and smoke some more.
Her physical pain goes away.
Feels like an empty shell.
Thinks the other side is better than this one.
She wishes she could cry.
Oh, how she has forgotten how?
Joy and happiness do not visit her.
She wishes for another life.
Tried to be a wife and mother.
Could not do either.
Her heart is still in cement.
Pain, fear and anger is still all she knows.

© KONINKLIJKE BRILL NV, LEIDEN, 2020 | DOI: 10.1163/9789004441651_019

Swallowing, snorting and smoking bring her too far down.
Is an adult, yet still feels like a child.
Scared an longing for real love,
Oh how she looks for a jackhammer to free her heart.
Praying to be freed and cured of her pain and her wounds healed.

CHAPTER 19

Everlasting Kiss

Jelisa Lovette

An everlasting kiss
A kiss that will last an eternity
Eternally in my mind, my thoughts
Of her still, immobile, silently reminiscing
Back to that moment of her and I.
Kissing for the very 1st time, in that place
Where kisses seem to last forever.
So to that moment I will forever
Remain chained.

Bound like a slave, I am to my memories
Of a kiss that will never die,
A kiss that only multiplies and
Turn into beautiful butterflies.
The feeling I feel so deep down inside
Of me, I feel on the surface of my
Skin.

I can see your words when you speak
To me in tongues with your lips that
Lingers on my tongue, baptized eternally
In an immortal kiss that never ends.

© KONINKLIJKE BRILL NV, LEIDEN, 2020 | DOI: 10.1163/9789004441651_020

CHAPTER 20

Backburner Bitch

Anonymous

Too busy to write,
Too tired to answer.
Pen to paper's not your thing,
But I knew this,
So that's on me,
You say.
How soon we forget
How I had you
Front and back
Way back
When you got left
By those
Who never looked back.
How soon we forget
The tears you dropped
From silence so loud,
From answerless questions
Twisting in the wind
By those with too many matters
For you to matter.
"Now I see what they mean,"
you say;
"It's not what it seems,"
you say;
     "Don't take this the wrong way,
     But you are on the back burner—
     That's reality."
You wanted our love to last,
You say,
And yet our love is last today.
Burned by the back
Of your agenda list,
I'm hurt, I'm mad, confused, and pissed.

© KONINKLIJKE BRILL NV, LEIDEN, 2020 | DOI: 10.1163/9789004441651_021

Demoted by distance
Conveniently switched
From love of your life,
To Backburner Bitch.

Twist me in the wind
Like leaves on a tree.
Forget, if you will.
What you know about me.

I'm built to last—
Not built to be last.

You twist me in the wind
'Cause you got it twisted.
Downgrading in the name
Of something to do.
Ten minutes to much
To get from you
While the weekend
You spend
With Houdini
Whose disappearing acts
Are still
A mystery to you.
But it's cool.
Facebook joyrides,
Anxious chihuahuas,
Cheap champagne,
And a.m. showers
Not alone.
Too busy
To answer your phone.
You've got us twisted;
My future's too bright for shade.

No bitch on this planet
Is built like me—
Cheap Champagne
You drink to my pain?
That's insane.

Diamonds for dirt
You tragically switch—
For a buzzard,
You give up
A quality bitch.

CHAPTER 21

Love Alive

Kala Keller

The sky is dark this morning when I raise my head. It isn't the first time I've had to rise out of dawn's ashes.

Every morning nowadays, I've been waking up early to finish an assignment. I get up and sit on my bed without a blanket, knowing I'll fall asleep if I stay warm. My shoulders are boulder-like, thick and frozen against the cool wall behind me. The draft in the room keeps my shoulders in check and my MacBook is icy against my bare thighs. I pull through though, like a goddamn Iditarod dog-wolf—only two more weeks and you're done with first semester, I keep telling myself. As I near the end of my memoir due for my first writing class (ever!), I pick my brain for the perfect title. I thought earlier in the morning that I could gift the memoir to my sister for Christmas at the end of the month, as the story was about our time together that summer in Seville. I couldn't wait for her to come back to America—she's currently on year two of her three-year Navy-wife tour de Europe. I decide on the title and save the document.

I look at my boyfriend, sleeping in our bed. I watch his bare chest rise and fall and his heavy breathing feels full in my ears. I think to myself that at any second his chest could burst right out and explode into a million pieces like a volcano. On the bedside table, come short vibrations. I roll my eyes. I wish Logan would just turn his game notifications off. The buzzing stops. I yawn. I close my computer.

Almost how thunder rolls through after lightning strikes, my phone begins to ring. I look at the clock—it's still not even 9 am yet. Mom's Cell. Yeah, it's definitely too early for that. I consider ignoring the call, but I don't.

"Is Logan with you?" she says.

"He's sleeping... did you just call him?" I say.

"Yes. I just wanted to make sure he was there."

... Is she drunk? I'm thinking.

"Daddy died, sweetie." she says. "He had a heart attack last night."

• • •

In the late winter afternoon, my sister and I split up some two hundred records, clad in blindfolds. We decided that his record collection would be the last thing we divided up, since they were what Dad valued the most. After a week of fumbling and sorting and fighting, we finally faced the last task. The decades-old vinyl records lied dusty on his closet shelf, and we both needed to reach for them on our tiptoes. As we began the blindfolded rummage, I cursed myself for not getting a pre-estimate on where my favorite records rested—all in healthy sisterly competition, of course. I sent my best energy towards what I knew I would listen to—the B52s classics, his favorite AC/DC albums, and most importantly, the five or six Heart records.

I had been cringing all week at those weathered Heart records—my father had been telling me for years before he died that I should look into the band. The group, he told me, consisted of two sisters—one sings, the other rocks the guitar. I never really looked them up, albeit once using their song "Magic Man" for an audition, but I made it my personal mission to get as many of their records as possible. I knew my sister wouldn't take the sob story as an excuse, so I had to just hope that they would rest in my hands at the end of the day.

Not surprisingly, it took more than an hour to move each record from its previous home on the shelf to one of two piles on the ground—Kelly's Pile and My Pile. Once the last record was pulled, we took our blindfolds off. I rushed to my stack. The first few records were unrecognizable to me, but I had faith that there were goodies hiding in the heap. One by one, I read them out loud. Some Jimi Hendrix, some Black Sabbath, some AC/DC (thank God). Right in the middle of the pile, I hit the jackpot. It was Little Queen. And then it was Bad Animals, then Bebe le Strange—almost all of his Heart albums, glowing in my lap.

• • •

Once, after my freshman year of college, I received a call from my dad.

"Do you wanna take a day trip tomorrow to Fox Lake? Your Uncle Bobby's boat is up for the summer, and he invited us to spend some time with him and your Aunt Sue."

My father picked me up just before 11. I felt silly for wearing my bathing suit so early on a Sunday morning, but nonetheless, I slipped my neon-green-and-yellow strapless dress over it and waited for pickup. If Kurtis A. Keller was notorious for anything, it was picking my sister and I up late. This time he was at least half an hour past schedule. We didn't have much to talk about during the forty-five minute car ride; in fact, we had very few things in common outside of Kelly and the everyday happenings of his work and my education. To save that precious talking juice for later, I told him I was feeling sleepy. He cranked up the radio.

By the time we hit the highway, all of the windows were down. I remember feeling immense pressure in my ears and the wind suffocated me a little. No longer pulled into a tight ponytail, my hair sliced my face and tickled my ears. I could sense the music from the radio in every part of me—buzzing in my toes, slapping the back of my neck. I knew all of the songs. My dad always had the same rock station on; personally, I'm convinced that there might not have even been any other presets on his radio. I can't even remember a time that my dad didn't have his own personal rock band following him around—at our backyard pool (while he taught four-year-old me to swim), in the basement with his friends over, and later at his apartment, where he shared a room with his glass-case Dolby surround sound record player. Even though I hated being dragged around to local festivals over my adolescent summers and hadn't fully adopted his knowledge of classic rock music, throughout my life I never denied my attraction to a hard-hitting and shameless beat.

While starting my research up for this project, I knew I wanted to focus on my dad's music. Though I had never experienced true grief, I had most definitely read one too many things about it, and figured that writing about how sad my dad's death made me would really just be an impersonal death treatise to everyone else. Wanting to avoid the cliché, I considered what it would be like to talk about the positive outcomes of his death (if you can call them positive). Ultimately, these were: 1) the music he left for me, and 2) the bunny he had to leave behind (but we will get to that later). While researching the musical connections between parent and child, I stumbled across something interesting.

An article titled "Intergenerational Continuity of Taste: Parental and Adolescent Music Preferences" from the journal Social Forces explains that a child's music preference is heavily influenced by his or her parents.' It theorizes that a person's taste in music is a sort of personality trait and that it can be viewed as a "rather stable characteristic of an individual" (Ter Bogt et al., 298). My father could not be a better example of this. Other than listening to his actual favorite bands, he had a plethora of AC/DC shirts, over 200 records of just rock music (seriously), and even a handful of recorded live-performance DVDs—he and his music go way back. When he died, almost every Facebook post commemorating him mentioned his love for rock music. So obviously, as a toddler, I was exposed to (if not spoon fed) that same legacy. Equally applicable, it is written on page 313, "girls may (turn) to their fathers and mothers' music collections and (assume) some of their parent's feelings for the genre." I knew I liked the way rock music made me feel, but I still would never have said it was my favorite genre. The past few months have changed that.

• • •

His whole life, my dad took care of rabbits. The first I know of was Dexter. Dexter had caramel fur and kind eyes, but he lived and passed before I was born. When I was a kid there was Moontan, whose white fur had black specs splattered down his spine. While packing up my dad's apartment, I found a few pictures of my sister and I with Moontan, even a video of us taking him for a walk in a harness. Moontan passed when I was in high school and my father was devastated. He told me on the phone that he felt empty, like he had nothing to come home to. Of course, my sister thought of the obvious solution: to gift my father a new baby bunny!

He was a sparky Netherland dwarf rabbit who looked like milk chocolate. His eyes were huge—they bulged out of his head like two dark marbles. He was tiny in my dad's big hands, and ran faster than the devil. Since my dad was a lifelong Looney Tunes fan, he named his new bunny Taz.

When my mom called to tell me my father died, she assured me that Taz was okay. Since she was allergic and couldn't immediately take care of him, the police department brought Taz to their temporary animal housing. Of course I didn't like the sound of that, but she insisted that there was no rush to come home and miss my finals. I didn't even have to volunteer myself to become Taz's new keeper—the whole family was already on board with having me adopt him.

Picking Taz up from the police station was the best day of my life. It ended up that the officer taking care of him had his own family bunnies and I felt comforted by his confidence as we walked into the dingy doghouse jail. He noticed my hesitation when I approached Taz's mini kennel, then joked with me that the whole station was tickled to see a 'bunny in custody.' After I half-heartedly reached my hand into the cage, the officer offered to help get Taz out. I stood in awe at the little creature as he was gently placed into my arms and I remember being very surprised at how light he was. His fur was delicate and simple, and as we walked out of the station, I suppressed a huge lump in my throat. This time, it wasn't from pain and grief. It was because, for the first time in three weeks, I felt happy.

• • •

After Christmas, my sister and I spent a couple of hours everyday clearing out my dad's apartment. Kelly's husband, Dylan, had been granted leave from his station in Spain and had been able to help us pack up for a week. He and Logan were the heavy lifters and our take-this-to-that boxers. Pretty much everything personal of my dad's was packed up at this point and only his furniture pieces still stood in their original spots.

It was Thursday. I was leaving the next day for an immersion back at Millikin and Kelly had already left with Dylan to visit his family for the holidays. I knew it was time to say goodbye to the apartment. I panicked about the room layout, knowing that in just a few more days, Kelly would remove the rest of the furniture and the apartment would be empty. So even though the layout hadn't changed in over ten years, I took a picture of his living room on my iPhone.

I looked through the records I won at the handoff the previous day. Pink Floyd, Tom Petty. All of the Heart records. And one that had gone unnoticed— Moontan, by a band called Golden Earring. It surprised me that I had never asked where the bunny's name came from. Sticking with my original favorite pick, I put Heart's Little Queen on his massive turntable. Logan and I sat on the infamously uncomfortable living room futon as Taz snuggled in my arms. The record was fuzzy for a few seconds before the music started, and I had no idea what to expect.

"Barracuda" was the first song on the album. My jaw dropped—I had no idea that the album had music on it I would recognize. I admired the album artwork—the Wilson sisters stand at some sort of Renaissance faire, clad in gypsy-garb. Nancy, the guitar player, holds a magic mirror of some sort, as Ann casts eyes like diamonds. In the back are the band members, also in mystical clothing, grouped next to a white horse and a literal goat. I couldn't stop saying, "Fierce! Fierce!"

After "Barracuda" finished, the album turned on its head. The second song was soft and somber, and an extended guitar melody breezed over my dad's turntable. It started gentle and spiritual, but eventually took a sort of groove. Ann's voice came again over my dad's old speakers, which were for sure at their volume capacity—the sky was dark this morning when I raised my head//ever since I was a baby girl, I wanted one thing most in this world... it was to keep my love, keep my love alive—and then with a hard bass drum kick, the full-band joined in. I had never heard anything like it.

After that night, all I wanted to listen to was Little Queen. I blasted it in the car, listened to it on my way to class, and used literally any excuse to bring it up to friends and family. I placed the record on a special shelf in my room, using it both as a conversation starter and as a centerpiece. It was actually in sharing this Heart obsession with my Critical Storytelling professor that she suggested I research how music connects us with the major chapters of our lives.

My initial searches on databases like JSTOR were all variants of (DEATH) and (ROCK MUSIC) and (SPIRITUALITY)). Nothing was coming up—seriously, the most applicable article I found was three pages on Chopin's Funeral March, titled "The Music of Death." I was so frustrated—why was I having such a hard time finding research that proved my dad was listening to the Heart record along with me? I knew I didn't want to research how music affected me cognitively and my topic was so layered that I came up empty-handed. Since it was still early in the semester, I momentarily gave up the search.

It took four months for me to find the right research. The concept of grief 'ritual' surfaced in an article I was reading about bereavement, and it opened up a whole new vein of understanding. According to C. Nancy Reeves, a psychologist from the University of Victoria, in Death Studies, "a death-related ritual is defined as a ceremony, directly involving at least 1 person and the symbols of the loss" (Reeves 408). Sounds obvious, right? In my grief process, I was absolutely using Heart to connect with my father. "The ritual involves heightened meaning and emotion and is often experienced as spiritual," Reeves says. She speaks of placing emotion into a symbol, writing that it "provides a forum where the death is acknowledged and accepted as real," and it "sets the climate for a potent honoring of the deceased" (Reeves 418). In the first month of grieving, I turned to the Heart record for light. It reminded me of the freedom my found dad in music, and in turn, I almost felt like I was setting him free.

• • •

Three days postpartum, my sister asked about the arrangements. "Have you thought about cremation?"

Even the thought of it sent shivers down my spine. Reluctantly, I replied.

"I read once about putting ashes into a tree and planting it? Something like that, could we do that?"

A pause. "It's definitely something to think about, for sure. I just don't know how cost effective it is." She continued, "We think the best option is cremation—It's the cheapest, and we could always sprinkle his ashes somewhere special! You know Daddy would have wanted the least-expensive option."

Her optimism seemed like a scam. Although he was a cheapskate at times, we both knew he loved being immersed in nature.

To bring it back, I asked, "Cost-effective, totally. What else will we end up having to pay for?"

"Dude, there's a lot. Like, seriously. There's arrangements—even without a funeral—there's the moving company, the rest of his rent, what to do with his cars. There's a lot we haven't discussed yet. I just didn't want to upset you, and I knew we could talk about it once we were all together."

"So you think the tree thing can't happen." I didn't hide my irritation.

"I didn't say that," she defended herself. "I'm just saying it's probably not reasonable."

And so I agreed to the cremation. As it was, I barely felt like there was a choice for my sister and me, but I was assured it was the right thing to do. Cremation is done all the time, who was I to prefer the most expensive option? I was uncomfortable with the fact that a funeral was too expensive for my dad's humble budget, but I understood there was nothing we could do about it, and I knew good would come out of the situation. It's the adult decision to save money and cremate him, right? Only a few people would have come to the funeral anyway. Michael Purcell couldn't have said it any better than in "Celebrating Death"—"So much needs to be arranged, and almost immediately the focus is shifted from the person who has died, and the pain which flows from that suddenly snapped relationship, to the practicalities which surround death" (684). Ninety percent of the time I was unable to tell if I was being reasonable with my family or if I was completely manic and unstable. I figured that I was being touchy about the whole thing just because I was, underneath it all, enduring incredible trauma. It drove me crazy that a funeral was out of the picture, but I needed to silence my true opinion so I could focus on making "reasonable" decisions regarding his post-death arrangements. Regardless, I couldn't shake the idea that I wouldn't be able to visit a grave on Father's Day.

Once the paperwork was processed, the cremation took a few days. On our last day of packing up the apartment, my sister and I drove together to pick up his ashes. Since we weren't planning to immediately bury them, we purchased two individual "keepsake urns." This way, we would still get all of his ashes, but a tiny bit would be placed aside into two mini-urns. They were $40 a pop, but you could choose what color velvet box you wanted, as well as the type of ceramic. I was glad that there was still something special we could get in place of a full-blown burial, and it's no surprise that my sister and I ended up ordering the same style in both box and urn—I like this, it's like each box is an equal part of him.

They left his watch with his ashes; apparently it was the only part of the remains that they couldn't cremate. Usually reluctant to hang on something sentimental like that, my sister took it out of the bag. It was below thirty outside and I couldn't feel my fingers, but the sight of it was comforting. She flipped the watch over, and revealed a caked and dirty underneath. We both laughed at that; my father's things always seemed to be grimy and sticky. He was a simple person and he didn't care too much about cleanliness.

As my sister and I pulled out of the funeral home parking lot, I felt weird about the urn in its little heart box. What will my friends think once it is on my shelf? What do I think about my dad as a fly on the wall? But I kept pushing myself to get over the social stigma bullshit and tried to appreciate that I had a portable piece of my dad. I let the urn into my life. I cleared an entire shelf off the bookcase in my room and made a shrine-like memorial for it. The open box stands proudly in the middle of the shelf and to either side of it there are classic pictures of my dad. I wanted to keep some of his possessions close to him, so I rummaged through the things of his that I kept and hand selected my favorites. He owned a surplus of bunny figurines, so I placed as many as I could fit on the shelf—I almost feel like they are his guardian bunnies.

I also started to take the urn places—a few times to the attic to listen to his records, once for a walk in the park. The Universe gave me a true handout in the spring and I actually saw Ann Wilson, the singer of Heart, in concert—all with my dad rolling around in my purse. The first song she sang was "Barracuda." I held my hand in my purse and coddled the urn during the concert. Upon returning the ceramic to its velvet home later that night, I connected the most obvious symbol: my dad is kept in a HEART. Just like the logo for the band, just like the beating of their drums, my dad's heart box pounded in the name of music and love.

I thought that, after time, I would stop thinking about his flesh being burned to ash. I never did.

> there is sweat
> dripping from the
> windows in the
> bathroom
> and my heart sags low
>
> in the other room my suitcase lies open
> its guts spill out into a
> hundred pink threads
> while the little red heart box
> tilts on its side
>
> running down the
> hall my throat starts
> to close my heart
> starts to swing back
> and forth
> back and forth
>
> I wait for the string to
> snap for my heart to splatter on the
> second-floor tile.

teardrops slip,
they are silent too

comfort comes from a
lover and his familiar
hands
there is warmth in his nest

but still,
I swore I just heard the
cry of the little red heart
box
Alone in the room down the hall
it tilts on its side
("Heart Box," 4/12/18)

• • •

This time the sky was clear and bright—it was early March, and the weather was starting to get a little kinder. I had walked across campus to an early Saturday morning event and was sitting in a meeting when my best friend tapped my arm.

Panic struck her face and she showed me her phone. A million texts from Logan:

Tell Kala to come home now.

Before I knew it, I was flying down the Shilling Hall stairs. When Logan answered his phone, he was crying so hard that I could barely understand him. Being shoved back to the loss of that cold December morning, I felt the same flash of shock. His mother died, I thought to myself. Oh god, not again.

"What's wrong, what happened?"

"Please come home, just come home." I was already running.

"Can you tell me what happened?" I tried to be gentle, but the hurt in his voice buckled in my knees.

"Taz is dead."

I couldn't breathe. My throat felt like it was closing in on itself—I was in such a state of shock that I couldn't even catch the thought to cry. But still, my eyes bulged wide with heavy rain, and, before I knew it, I was home. I could hear Logan from outside the house.

Walking up the stairs, I felt reality twisting and contorting. An overwhelming sense of collapse rose in my chest and I swear that my breathing stopped completely. But it wasn't until I opened the bedroom door that my heart actually broke. Logan sat hunched over on the bed. He was rocking back and forth, enveloping the rabbit completely. He had swaddled Taz in his favorite fleece blanket and held him like a child. Floods of compassion spilled down his cheeks as he cradled the lifeless bunny and we all held each other for a long time before even saying a word. I consider this to be our first real family hug.

We knew we had to bury him and we had the perfect place in mind. Even though I hadn't stopped crying, I started to shove some of Taz's belongings into my purse: his favorite toy, a bag of hay, some pellets. I grabbed a Polaroid of Logan holding him and another of him and me. I went to the pictures I have of my dad and carefully selected one.

Logan let me hold Taz on the car-ride there. It was such a nice Saturday afternoon, as I got out of the car I could feel the sun shining. We walked until we reached the perfect spot. It was on a hill overlooking the woods, and right behind it was the most magnificent tree I had ever seen. I started to talk with Taz, telling him about his new bed in the ground and introducing him to the nature around him. Logan began to dig a hole with a plastic hand shovel, and, once that cracked in half, he finished the rest with his fists. At a certain point, though, he couldn't dig any deeper—roots from the tree obstructed his way. Turns out, that exposed root was the perfect cocoon for our sweet bunny. With his head on the root and the rest of his body curling right into place, this seemingly impossible nook became Taz's final resting spot.

After putting all of his favorite things with him, Logan and I packed the dirt back over Taz. It was incredibly difficult to do, but I knew that Mother Nature was about to reclaim one of her many sons. Once the hole was covered, Logan and I sat nearby for a long time, sharing memories. I thanked Taz for being there for me after my dad's death. I thanked him for being with my dad as he passed. I mentioned that my dad was probably even there with us, and that he was beaming to reunite with his bunny. I closed my eyes. I saw my dad sitting behind me, right in front of the tree. I was doubtful at first that I didn't just make it up, but then I actually saw him reach out to me. I felt his firm grip on my shoulder, and I felt warm and safe and validated. The tears I had accumulated for Taz stopped for a moment and all I could focus on was my dad's touch. Out of nowhere a hummingbird started to chirp and the feeling was gone.

Always a strong believer in animal messengers, I looked up the hummingbird's significance, and here's some trivia for you: the hummingbird's wings flutter in an infinity symbol. They represent eternity, as well as endurance, and according to article "Wintering Hummingbirds in Alabama and Florida: Species Diversity, Sex and Age Ratios, and Site Fidelity," they can travel over 1,000 kilometers during migration (Basset & Cubie, 2009, p. 158). It's clear to me that during the moment with my father, Taz migrated to his lightest form of being. He was welcomed with sunshine and escorted to his finest heaven. The hummingbird was his careful guide, and of course my dad followed by closely. I am certain that all three of them work on the moon together.

$$\bullet\bullet\bullet$$

Bruce Fogel, a veterinarian from England, says "the death of a pet is often the trigger for a double mourning, as if somehow the quality of that relationship released grief about a human loss which was not felt at the time" (Noonan 405). It took me until May to realize the parallel between Taz's death and my father's. I had been doing alright for the three months in between, seeing a counselor for grief management, keeping up with my family, finding my own ways to cope. Once Taz died, however, I felt like I relapsed completely into grief's viper fangs. I've had dogs in the family my whole life—Luna's death in fifth grade was unbearable, don't get me wrong—but Taz's death was the first time in my life that I had to bury something I loved. I had grown with and treasured my time Taz and he was there with my dad when he passed. I had always seen Taz as an extension of my father's amber energy and having to bury his beautiful light was heartbreaking.

Still, I will always remember Taz's burial as a beautiful offering, as a return to nature. There was a ceremony—a classic ritual—to commemorate his life and thank him for his impact. It was messy and painful, but it was a graceful exchange and transcendence of energy. A hummingbird honored us, and my father visited and gave thanks. In the following weeks we mourned our loss, but Logan always reminded me, "Taz is having so much fun running around the forest, the hummingbird is watching him, he has pellets and toys with him." He didn't make the choice himself, but it was obvious that Taz would return to the ground once he passed—that's what people do with animals.

When my father died, I had to make decisions about his "arrangements." I had to sign the Humes Funeral Home packet, check which box: Traditional Funeral Service, at the price of $6,200, or the Direct Cremation Package, at the much cheaper clearance-like rate, $2800 ("General Price List"). I literally had to choose which fucking box to put my dad in. Perhaps it's at the fault of the funeral home, whose costs were too high. Maybe it's secretly the government profiting on the most vulnerable humans in the country. Who knows what—in my situation, burial wasn't an option, and a funeral would have cost more than it was worth. The understood ritual of the funeral and burial was taken away from me and it was replaced by its socially acceptable standby, cremation and an urn. Although this "arrangement" is perfect for some people, I found out that it disturbed my personal mourning process.

Without a funeral, my father's post-death arrangements seemed kind of... abnormal. Never in my life have I had a problem with the idea of cremation, but when it came to my father's arrangement, something about it was anticlimactic and unresolved. There was no obvious transcendence like with Taz's death, no hummingbird to carry my father to heaven. Adele M. Fiske reviews a possible source for this dissonance in "Death: Myth and Ritual"—she suggests "the funeral ritual itself, a technique, (deals) with the mysterious and disturbing phenomenon of death." She says, "all rituals have a common element, an initiatory essence, death followed by "resurrection" (Fiske 249–50). I went through a short religious phase in high school, but the idea of "resurrection" means something else for me. In my opinion, it's shape shifting in a way— moving from flesh to spirit, from past life to next life. And, each time I engage with one of my rituals, even including those concerning the mini-urn, I believe I am helping my dad in his long-term transition. Resurrection, to me, signifies eternal life—not with God, but instead with the Universe and with nature. Even though my father's flesh is gone, his love still breathes. It never died.

My father passed down a playful passion for rabbits, leaving a legacy. A month or so after Taz's death, Logan and I adopted a new, young, and fuzzy bunny. We named him Marko—the 'k' for Keller. My ever-growing relationship with Marko, I believe, allows my father's love to live. Likewise, appreciating his favorite music connects me to the part of me that is him. When I take time to be present in nature, he is there with me. These rituals are the natural, spiritual responses to my father's death—they were coping mechanisms as much as they were personal discoveries and I would not have been able to work through my grief without them. Yeah, I know I wanted to avoid the "grief" talk. As I said, I thought writing about my grief would have been impersonal for all of the people who weren't me. But while researching it, I discovered the power of ritual. And in the final circumstances of his cremation, I was able define my own understanding of death and resurrection.

But what was most confusing was realizing that at times, I was alone. My reaction to my father's death was frequently more dramatic than my sister's. I would cry a lot one week and then not at all the next. My sister probably wasn't completely overanalyzing her little mini-urn, taking it with her to different places in Europe and writing poems about it. She wasn't even engaging with his music until a few months later, when she bought a beautiful wooden record player. She grieved in other ways; she had her own rituals. Turns out, there isn't a one-size-fits-all way to grieve—each person needs to develop their own approach. So, I don't think I was having an issue with accepting my father's death. I think the issue lied in accepting the love in the ways I was grieving.

A poem by Linda Pastan puts it well: "Grief is a spiral staircase." For a semester I have been stepping in and out of an ever-changing staircase, never actually getting to the end. As I write this almost five months from my dad's death, I can still see his smile. Engaging with past memories still drains me of emotion, and I still catch myself saying, "he is" instead of "he was." Even though I felt it the day he died and every morning for weeks after, sometimes I can still feel my heart break for the first time. It will happen while I open my trunk, while I'm washing a dish or cleaning my desk. But it took me a long time to realize that it's just a part of my love; it's just a part of my process. My duty, as half of his kin and a holder of his heart, is to keep his love flowing, and sometimes, my heart overflows too.

And so I listen to his music. I take care of Marko. I giggle at the awkward voicemails he used to leave me, and I look through pictures that make me smile. I share the story of my dad's life, good and bad, with my loved ones, and

I talk with him through the veiled porcelain moon. The love I share with my father has always been there—like the blood that pumps through my veins and the bass drum that kicks in my ears, he is a part of me. He is with me. He is in the porcelain urn and in the wind thrashing through my car windows. He laughs with me when Marko jumps and jitters and he dances under the needle of my record player. His love is wild and free. It's not my fault that "ever since I was a baby girl, I wanted one thing most in this world." It was, and always will be, to keep my love—keep his love alive.

References

Bassett, F., & Cubie, D. (2009). Wintering hummingbirds in Alabama and Florida: Species diversity, sex and age ratios, and site fidelity. *Journal of Field Ornithology, 80*(2), 154–162.

Fiske, A. M. (1969). Death: Myth and ritual. *Journal of the American Academy of Religion, 37*(3), 249–265.

Heart. (1977). *Love alive.* Kaye Smith Studios.

Noonan, E. (2008). People and pets. *Psychodynamic Practice, 14*(4), 395–407. doi:10.1080/14753630802492722

Reeves, N. C. Death acceptance through ritual. *Death Studies, 35*(5), 408–419. doi:10.1080/07481187.2011.552056

Ter Bogt, T. (2011). Intergenerational continuity of taste: Parental and adolescent music preferences. *Social Forces, 90*(1), 297–319.

The music of death. (2016). The Lotus Magazine, 8(3), 116–118.

CHAPTER 22

My Dragonfly

Laura Nearing

Baby Nearing, born September 27, 1999. The day I became a big sister and pushed to the sidelines. I only have one sibling, my brother, but I'm two and a half years older than him. I was used to being the center of attention, but when my brother was born, he captured all of that attention that was usually on me. I retaliated in quirky ways that my mom shares with me to this day—her favorite is when I peed on the floor in front of where she was changing my brother's diaper—but my retaliation came from a place of jealousy. Three and four-year-old me wasn't used to having to share attention, and it was something that I held against my brother, although it wasn't anybody's fault.

Every time family would come over they would want to see the baby and play with the baby and hold the baby and watch the baby, and I would stay in my room and hide under my bed, reading books. My Uncle Eric was different. I didn't have to resort to my usual antics when family came around, as long as he was there. He spent time with my brother, but he made the extra effort to hang out with me too. He used to take me up and down the block on his Harley, and it felt like the best thing in the world. I loved the powerful rumbling underneath me, I used to close my eyes and pretend I was riding in the middle of a herd of horses. My brother was never allowed to ride the Harley, probably because he was just a little too small, but it made me feel special. The Harley and its power was something only we shared.

We had an incredibly close bond. Every time we had a family party, he would ride his motorcycle over. I don't have any memories of him driving a car, only riding his Harley Davidson. Once I heard the tell-tale rumbling of his "Dream-cycle," I would run out to the driveway and jump into his arms. He always had a joke for me, something cheesy, but something that made me laugh until my stomach hurt regardless. I remember one day he came over and I was wearing a pair of navy shorts that said "STAR" on the back. He kept reading it backwards, asking why I had the word "RATS" on my butt. It was absolutely cheesy and ridiculous, but as a kid I thought it was the funniest thing in the world. That's probably why I remember that moment to this day.

Once, he came over to visit when I was probably around five years old. My mom, brother, my Uncle Eric, and I were all sitting in the family room, and, as usual, I was trying to turn some of the attention on me. I was brushing my hair but thought it would be funny if I turned the brush around to pretend to brush with the smooth side. The back of the purple brush hit my head a little too hard, and it drew tears to my eyes. I remember feeling so embarrassed, but Uncle Eric walked over, gently removed the brush from my hand, and placed me on his lap, reminding me I didn't have to turn to those antics with him around.

My Uncle Eric always smelled like patchouli. He never wore any other cologne, only patchouli. When Christmas came around, me and my cousins would always smell the presents under the tree to figure out which ones were from him. He never put a sticker with his name on it because it was one of our favorite traditions, smelling all the presents. One year I asked for a bottle of my own patchouli for Christmas, and he was the one that bought it for me. It was one of my favorite presents that year.

I never had to pretend to be anything else but myself around Uncle Eric. He always made me feel loved, accepted, and important. He had one of the biggest impacts on my life when I was younger. He was my hero. My 6'4", bearded, Harley-riding, patchouli-scented hero.

• • •

When does grieving really end? Will I forever grieve, or will it turn into sadness at some point? Will I be sad until I leave this murky pond and join my dragonflies above water? Or will I learn to accept this murky pond as my home for now, and trust that my dragonflies are not hovering too far?

• • •

My Uncle Eric was hit and killed by a drunk driver when I was in fifth grade. He was riding his motorcycle—his DreamCycle—home from playing pool with my Uncle Mark, when a lady who was in too much of a rush swerved out of her lane to avoid a red light and broadsided him.

He died on the ambulance ride to the hospital.

The entire right side of his body was crushed to smithereens. I remember because we couldn't hug him during the funeral, even though it was an open casket. Daddy had to pull Eric's fiancée away from his body. She was hugging him too hard and his body, pumped with toxins to preserve him, might have collapsed. The day that it happened, my dad was extra nice to me and my brother. I mean, he's always nice, but that day seemed a little different. I didn't know why, but I didn't question it. My parents had just divorced, maybe less than a year before—maybe over two years before, I'm not exactly sure—and it was his night for visitation.

He drove me and my brother home. I remember pulling up next to our driveway because we couldn't pull in, there were so many cars. They completely filled our driveway and were up and down both sides of the street. I saw family and friends bringing in platters of food and fruit trays. I was so excited. I thought we were having a party. My exact words when I entered the house were, "Are we having a fiesta?!"

I was so, so wrong. My mom was there, smiling in the strangest way. "No, honey. We have to talk."

• • •

One Sunday, a few years after Uncle Eric had passed, my mom and I were speeding down the streets of our neighborhood. We were late to church. It was warm, sunny, and spring. As we drove through our forested streets, we stopped briefly at a stop sign, and a bright blue dragonfly landed on the hood of our car. My mom stopped, looking at it. I told her to hurry up, we were late, but she just stopped and stared.

"Dragonflies remind me of my brother, you know?" She said softly, smiling.

I was confused for a second, wondering why. My Uncle Eric was a strong, manly, biker, not a dainty little dragonfly. I asked her why. She pulled through the stop sign and parked on the side of the street.

"I'm going to tell you one of my favorite stories. Once upon a time, there was a water bug that lived in the bottom of a peaceful pond filled with lily pads and surrounded by tall green grass. The water bug and his friends were inseparable, they loved nothing more than to dart between the long, thick stems of the pads that clouded the bottom of the pond like clouds on a sunny day. Every time a water bug climbed to the top of those long, thick stems, they never returned back to the bottom of the pond. They always pondered, wondering about their friends' safety. Are they okay? Did they forget about us? Eventually, they would move on and continue to enjoy the warm pond.

One day, it was time for the water bug to make his way to the top of the water. He didn't know what would happen to him, but he knew it was the right time. He felt at peace, ready to make the journey. He said goodbye to his friends and promised to come back down to visit them and tell them what it was like above water. Slowly, he made his way up from the dark, muddy bottom of the pond to the sunny, bright, warm surface of the water.

As he emerged, the water bug turned into a beautiful dragonfly. He spread his wings and took off into the clear, crisp sky. The sun was so warm, the air so pure, the life so vibrant. He never realized life could be this beautiful. As a water bug, he only knew the dark depths of his small pond. As a dragonfly, he is free to explore the world around him, full of vivid colors and swirls of sound and rich smells.

After enjoying his new surroundings, he remembered the promise he made to his friends. He couldn't wait to tell them how beautiful life was when he left the bottom of his muddy pond. He spread his wings, preparing to dive to the bottom of the pond. Bounce. He deflected from the surface. Bounce. Bounce. Bounce bounce bounce. Try as he might, he couldn't make it past the reflective surface of the rippling water.

As he hovered over the surface, he could see his beloved friends darting between the thick stems of the lily pads that cover the surface of his pond. Although he was sad to have to say goodbye to his friends for now, he took consolation in the fact that soon, his friends would become dragonflies too. When that time came, they would be able to fly all over the beautiful world that is above water. In the meantime, although they can't see him, and although they miss him, he will always be nearby, hovering over the water and watching over his friends."

By the end of the story, the dragonfly had left, but my Uncle Eric was still there. I felt him, connected to me by the story. He was my mother's dragonfly, and now he was mine too.

• • •

As I was brainstorming different topics of research to include in my paper, I immediately thought of grief. Everybody has their own idea of grief, but I don't think many people understand the psychological definition of grief, or at least I didn't. I combed through different articles and different sites until I stumbled across a phrase: complicated grief. I googled the definition and what I found on Mayo Clinic stunned me.

Complicated grief is described as grief that is prolonged, severe, and difficult to recover from. Complicated grief is also known as persistent complex bereavement disorder. People who suffer from complicated grief often have difficulty accepting the reality of their loss, allowing themselves to experience the pain of their loss, adjusting to a new reality in which the deceased is no longer present, and having other relationships. Common symptoms of complicated grief include intense sorrow and pain, focusing on little else but your loved one's death, extreme focus on reminders of the loved one or excessive avoidance of reminders, problems accepting the death, numbness or detachment, bitterness about your loss, and lack of trust in others.

I read through the symptoms list, mentally creating a checklist. Check, check, check, and check. Then, I had the most bizarre feeling of guilt. I thought maybe I was being dramatic, maybe I didn't experience complicated grief. After all, it wasn't a parent who died. After all, all of the examples of complicated grief I was finding included parents or significant others or children. Nothing about an uncle. But, the symptoms didn't lie. It took me about 10 years to realize it, but when my uncle died, I began to suffer from complicated grief.

• • •

When I received the news, I was numb. I've never actually felt numb before, and I don't think I've felt that way since. But I was so, so numb. I cried, but so silently. My mouth was shut, I was silent, but the tears wouldn't stop leaking out of my eyes. It didn't seem real, like it was a joke. How could this have happened?

Why him?

I sat on the couch for a long time. The rest of my family began to trickle into the kitchen to make funeral plans. I assume other people were crying as well, but it only felt like me. I was only aware of myself.

I don't remember anything of the next few weeks. Family from upstate New York flew in, but I don't remember if anybody stayed at our house or not. I don't remember how soon they flew in or even when they left. The funeral may have been a few days after or a few weeks after, I'm not sure. It's strange how memory works. How does your brain decide what's important to keep and what isn't?

• • •

According to Paul King, a neuroscientist from UC Berkeley Redwood Center for Theoretical Neuroscience, there are several different factors that determine what memories your brain stores. These factors include repetition, primacy and recency, surprise, emotional impact, and positive and negative outcomes.

Julia Lundstrom reported an article that found that short-term memory was affected for all the study participants experiencing grief, and for those that experienced complicated grief, memory was impacted even more. Those suffering from complicated grief could remember almost anything if the memory involved the lost loved one, and memories not included the loved one were severely impacted.

According to this article, the "memory issues" (I hate that word—"issues"), usually go back to normal (I also hate that word—"normal") after the person has completely grieved, and the timeline differs for each person. It made me think. Am I still grieving? Or have I completed my grieving stage? I'm not sure what finishing grieving would feel like, but I know that sometimes the sadness is still so deep and so fresh, and years later I still cry over the loss of him.

• • •

I don't remember very many things about my uncle's funeral, but what I do remember is vivid. I remember the two dresses I wore. For the wake, I wore a black and white striped dress. The fabric was ruched, so it looked like some of the stripes were raised while others lay flat. I remember for the funeral my dress was plain black except for a white band around my waist. My mom bought both of them for me. I don't remember why I didn't go shopping with her.

I remember the day of the wake, standing in a line for hours while people who I didn't know would hug me, shake my hand, pat my shoulder. I remember being upset for some reason, like who the hell are they to be sad? He was my uncle. He was my best friend.

I remember my dad waiting patiently in line, walking up to me and giving me a hug. I remember thinking it was weird. My mom was standing in the family line next to her boyfriend, now my step dad, whom I only met a few days ago, and my dad is the one having to wait to offer his condolences. I felt like my dad should have been the one standing next to my mom. I now love my stepdad very deeply and am so thankful for his presence on that day, but at the time, it was another source of anguish for me.

I remember stealing away to the kitchen with my cousins, trying to avoid the constant crying and tissues and tears and sniffles and I'm sorrys. My cousin had a brand new, bright green iPod shuffle. We listened to Fergalicious on repeat. Every time a family member or friend or acquaintance came over to offer their "I'm *so so* sorry"s, we would alternate who would answer them. "It's your turn," we would say as someone came over to our table with sad eyes and hugs. It was almost like reading from a script, the other person had to remember their lines and we had to remember ours. It was too much for four little kids to handle themselves, it took all of us to get through all the sympathies.

I feel like I remember more from the day of the funeral. I remember the room being so crowded that people were pressed up against each other. I remember the powerful grumbling of hundreds of Harley Davidsons idling in the parking lot. I remember walking up to the podium to share a story about my uncle—how I was always able to tell what Christmas presents were his by the strong smell of patchouli—and having to be walked back to my seat because of my hysterical sobbing. I remember the chorus of bagpipes playing Amazing Grace. I can't listen to Amazing Grace to this day without getting emotional.

The image that sticks out so clearly in my head is of my Uncle Mark, one of the strongest men I know, walking up to his brother's casket to lay a pine branch on his body, and falling to his knees, wailing. I remember my grandmother mourning her son who was buried in the ground before her. I remember the unfairness, the unjustness, the wrongness of it all.

How was the drunk driver, this selfish, unremorseful, self-centered woman, able to get away with causing this much pain? How could she kill someone, rip the pillar out of a family, and end up with only a slap on the wrist?

• • •

The CDC reports that every day in the United States, 29 people die in car accidents involving a drunk driver. In 2016 that number was 10,497 people. In 2008, 11,773 people died in accidents involving a drunk driver. My uncle was one of those deaths.

I desperately wish that number was 11,772 deaths instead. Even if it was, that means that 11,772 other families in the US alone had to deal with the same grief, the same funerals, the same dreaded phone call that changed their lives forever. I read that number, 11,773, and thought God. It's so high. How could it be so high? How can year after year after year thousands and thousands of people die and thousands more deal with crushing grief, and nothing changes?

This number must decrease. Year after year, thousands of people are killed by drunk drivers and the number hardly seems to waver. I believe one of the most powerful ways to decrease this number is to raise awareness. People have the incredible ability to sympathize and empathize, and that should be used to gain awareness of this massive issue. I feel it is my duty to share my story in order to demonstrate the devastating effects of drunk driving deaths. I know that I will never drive even slightly intoxicated or share a car with a drunk driver, and if I could just influence a couple people to make that same decision, it makes a difference.

That lady, the drunk driver that killed my uncle, was one of the thousand drunk drivers that took a valuable life that year. The most fucked up thing is that her daughter was in the car with her. This woman killed a man, a kind and gentle man, and her daughter had to witness it. Her daughter has to live the rest of her life knowing that her mother killed a man because she was in too much of a rush to wait for a light and she was in too much of a rush to wait until the alcohol left her system.

I hope the mother feels that guilt every day. I'm a Christian, and I believe in the power of forgiveness, but I'm not there yet. Even as I sit here typing this, my hands are shaking with anger. My mother has forgiven her, and every time I ask her how it is possible, why did she forgive this woman, she answers "It's the only way I'm able to move on."

I don't know, maybe I'm not ready to move on and forgive and forget. I feel like this anger may be the only thing connecting me to my uncle.

• • •

It took me a while to think about my uncle without immediately bursting into tears. I'm not sure if that qualifies as "recovering," but for me it felt like some small progress. I can't imagine how the rest of my family was feeling in the following months, and I feel guilty for not considering them at the time. Eventually, I returned to school and life resumed as usual. Most of my friends and teachers were genuinely sorry for my loss, but others had that uncomfortable sense of sympathy, the kind where they feel awkward around the topic, feel slightly sad for me, but are also glad that it didn't happen to them. I wish I was in their shoes.

• • •

As I was performing research for my story, I initially looked at how grief of a loss affects childhood development. The problem is, all of the papers were about the loss of a parent or sibling. As I combed through database after database, I could feel my frustration growing and surmounting.

There is almost no research about loss of an important family member like an aunt or uncle or cousin. Why is there such a difference between parents and uncles? I understand the biological difference, but why should that affect if and how long someone should grieve? Why is one type of grief more important than the other? Does my grief for my uncle not matter when in comparison to grief for a parent?

I experienced this conflict years after my uncle's death, and even to this day. My boyfriend isn't very close to his extended family, so he doesn't quite understand. He sympathizes, but only to a certain extent, and I get the impression that he thinks I may be overreacting at times. To be fair, I do tend to overreact occasionally, but this is a loss that still affects me deeply.

For some reason, people tend to think that if you aren't losing a parent or sibling, that the loss isn't as significant. I think any loss is significant if you loved them. Research should not exclude grief of a loved one because they aren't your father, mother, brother, or sister. Any sudden, unexpected death of a dearly loved one causes a massive amount of grief, and research should reflect that.

• • •

- "Childhood adversities and depression: I. Effects of early parental loss on the rearing behaviour of the remaining parent."
- "Childhood parental bereavement: The risk of vulnerability to delinquency and factors that compromise resilience."
- "Parental death during childhood and subsequent school performance."

The list continues. Paper after paper described childhood bereavement in relation to a parent, never an uncle. The trends were all the same, though. Children who had lost a parent were more troubled, performed poorly in school, were more inclined to delinquency, and were more closed off. Basically, if you had lost a parent, your childhood was screwed.

• • •

As I was reading my draft to a friend, she said something that resonated with me. "Validate your own grief." She was right.

All of my research and reactions from teachers and family and friends had taught me that for some reason, as long as I didn't lose a parent, I shouldn't grieve for long. 10 years later, I still grieve, and after writing and sharing my story, I realize that's okay. I don't grieve all of the time and I don't feel sad all of the time, but when I do, I don't need research or the approval of others to validate my emotions.

My grief reflects my deep love for my uncle. He was my role model, my best friend, and a father figure. Losing him left a deep scar, one that hasn't quite healed yet and may never fully heal. Until it does, I will not hide from my grief and sadness, but instead embrace it and share it, because by sharing my grief I am also sharing the stories of my uncle that make me smile and laugh and remind me of sunny days and rumbling Harleys and green ponds with blue dragonflies.

My Uncle Eric is my dragonfly. He reminds me of what it means to love and lose and gain strength from that love and loss. He is never far away, and always a part of me. The tattoo on my neck reminds me of that every day. Every time I smell patchouli or hear the tell-tale roar of a Harley or see a dragonfly, I smell, hear, and see my Uncle Eric, and a gentle touch to the back of my neck tells me he's here, he's protecting me, and he will always love me. Though cut short, I am grateful for the time we had together, as it has shaped me and molded me into the strong young woman I am.

I will love you forever, Uncle Eric. I can't wait to see you above water.

References

Berg, L., Rostila, M., Saarela, J., & Hjern, A. (2014). Parental death during childhood and subsequent school performance. *Pediatrics, 133*(4), 682–689. doi:10.1542/peds.2013-2771

Centers for Disease Control and Prevention. (2017, June 16). *Impaired driving.* Retrieved from https://www.cdc.gov/motorvehiclesafety/impaired_driving/impaired-drv_factsheet.html

Draper, A., & Hancock, M. (2011). Childhood parental bereavement: The risk of vulnerability to delinquency and factors that compromise resilience. *Mortality, 16*(4), 285–306. doi:10.1080/13576275.2011.613266

Edgar Snyder & Associates. (n.d.). *Past drunk driving accident statistics: 2011 and earlier.* Retrieved from https://www.edgarsnyder.com/drunk-driving/past-drunk-driving-statistics.html

King, P. (2016, April 6). How does the human brain decide which memories to store? *Quora.* Retrieved from https://www.quora.com/How-does-the-human-brain-decide-which-memories-to-store

Kitamura, T., Sugawara, M., Toda, M. A., & Shima, S. (1998). Childhood adversities and depression: Effects of early parental loss on the rearing behaviour of the remaining parent. *Archives of Women's Mental Health, 1*(3), 131–136.

Lundstrom, J. (2016, April 29). Good grief: How mourning can affect your memory. *Simple Smart Science.* Retrieved from www.simplesmartscience.com/good-grief-how-mourning-can-affect-your-memory/

Osterweis, M., Solomon, F., & Green, M. (1984). *Bereavement: Reactions, consequences, and care.* Institute of Medicine (US) Committee for the Study of Health Consequences of the Stress of Bereavement. National Academies Press.

CHAPTER 23

Puzzle Pieces in My Eyes

Rebekah M. Icenesse

My mother always told me I was beautiful. It seemed like almost every day she said that to me. "You're so beautiful." Hearing those three words repeated daily and feeling the love behind each syllable, I knew I had a great support system. I knew that I was beautiful. I didn't have any reason to think otherwise. Even when I had red acne spots covering my entire face and crooked teeth that would not touch until braces were put on, I knew I was still loved and beautiful in my mom's eyes. My mom has always been my hero. Growing up in a house-hold that was half boys, she was the only other girl with me, and she taught me how to be a strong and independent woman.

I was born into a Christian family that went to church three or four times a week and prayed over every meal. I was dedicated and baptized in a Pente-costal church and grew up knowing all about God and Jesus. I would sing the church songs and raise my hand during praises with my parents by my side. I never had any doubts or concerns about my family and my life. We created fun memories and were always happy spending time together making memorable experiences.

My parents played a big role in my life. I looked to them as examples for how I should act in adulthood and how to be an overall successful human being. They could sometimes be strict on academics and behavior, and I couldn't do some of the immature things that my friends were allowed to do. I was a naive child, who did not experience any tough love or pain. I had two parents who loved me unconditionally, and I never had to see the life problems with which my parents dealt. My parents gave me the childhood they never had, and I am grateful for the strong relationship I have with my family. We were one unit who never let each other fall. Even when we did fall, we'd pick each other up, which made us even stronger. I thought my family was so solid that nothing could ever hurt us. Seeing light and happiness in my family all my life, I didn't realize it could easily become dark and painful. I never thought that I would experience what helplessness felt like—heartache. I was 12 years old when my mother told me that she had Breast Cancer. My life was changed forever.

•••

© KONINKLIJKE BRILL NV, LEIDEN, 2020 | DOI: 10.1163/9789004441651_024

It was a hot summer day in June 2010. I was on summer break, about to become a seventh grader, and I had spent the first part of the summer swimming in pools, running around the neighborhood with the other neighbor kids, and staying up late. I went to my hip-hop dance classes every Monday. At home during the week, I practiced at home for our recital routine that my studio put on at the end of the month. As an eleven year old, I thought I was living the life. I had my friends that I saw every day, I was getting better at memorizing my dance routines, and I was taking fun adventures to St. Louis with my family. Everything was normal.

I woke up one morning and did my usual daily summer routine. At ten o'clock, I rose to the light streaming through the curtains hung around my bedroom windows, sunlight illuminating my room with a soft pink glow. After pulling myself out of my twin bed, I walked down the hallway and into the kitchen to grab a pop tart. When I got my blueberry pop tart, I went back to my room, sat on my bed and stared aimlessly—pop tart in hand—at my 20 inch television that played Cloudy with a Chance of Meatballs. I watched the movie that I had seen too many times before, and waited for the clock on my bedside table to turn to eleven o'clock. Once the red numbers flashed eleven, I immediately grabbed my small red cell phone and called my neighborhood friends, who were brothers. I asked them if they wanted to play, which they did. So I put on my jean shorts and aeropostale t-shirt and told my dad I was going over their house to play.

I saw the duo almost every day, and we always played pretend games, walked in the trails behind our subdivision, or rode our bikes and had races around the neighborhood block. Our block was basically a big circle, with most houses filled with retired teachers from the school district. I spent the entire day playing games over at their house, located a few houses over from mine, and left around four so they could eat dinner. When I arrived back home, I sat down on one of the brown leather couches in my basement with my older brother and waited until I could go back over and keep playing. Everything appeared ordinary and normal.

Then my front door opened, and my mother came inside.

I was too busy staring at the T.V. to hear anything my parents said upstairs, but, ten minutes after my mother got home from work, my brother and I were called upstairs. When we went up the stairs and into the kitchen, the entire atmosphere in the house changed. My mom stood on one side of the room, near the kitchen sink, and my dad stood on the other side, near the kitchen table. From the looks on both of their faces, I knew instantly that something was wrong. There was a moment of silence and then my mom started to tell us that she had recently been to the doctor's. She paused and looked at my dad. Her lips trembled and tears sprang from her eyes.

"Honey, I could have told them," my dad tried to comfort her and the tears kept on flowing.

Through all of her cries, she chokes out, "I have Breast Cancer."

• • •

I feel cold. My body goes numb, and I can't focus on anything but one spot on the wall behind the kitchen sink. No. This can't be happening. I drown out the heavy sobs that are ringing in my ears, and I only feel my heart racing, almost beating out of my small chest. I don't know whether to bawl or scream until my voice goes mute. I feel like I'm not in my body anymore—that I have drifted away and am looking at the entire room as if it were in a movie on the television screen. I don't know how long I stood there motionless, but my vision blurs and I take a heavy breath. My cheeks feel wet, but I don't move to dry them. I can't stop the tears, and all I can do is repeat the four words over and over again inside my head.

"I have Breast Cancer."

I feel an embrace, and it registers to me that I am being hugged. I don't even remember putting my arms around my mother and holding her with a tight grip. Maybe if I hold on tight enough, this sickness will go away. Please go away. Please don't take my mother away. I didn't realize before how easy life can be taken away. One month ago, my mother was healthy and happy, especially when she saw me blow out the '12' candles on my birthday cake. Now she's dying and there is nothing I can do to stop it. My mind keeps spinning in circles, and I can barely hear the sad mumbles.

"We'll get through this together as a family. Everything will be alright." I close my eyes.

Please leave. Please don't take my mother away.

• • •

My mouth felt like cotton and my heart ached. I wiped the hot tears away and gave my mom one last hug. As we hugged, she told me that we are not blaming God for this. I was confused. How could he let this happen? Why would this happen to her, of all people? My mom is the most generous and empathetic person and never asks for anything in return. I thought that she resembled a rose. She is beautiful, loving, and delicate, but has thorns that would come out and cause pain if she ever feels threatened. She is strong and perennial—she continues to grow back every year, even when the world gives her reasons not to.

My mom works her butt off in her career and never receives the same respect that she always gives. In my twelve-year-old eyes, she is (and still is) the world's greatest mother, and I did not want to lose her to this illness. But not even her own thorns could take this away.

According to U.S. Breast Cancer Statistics, "About 1 in 8 U.S. women (about 12.4%) will develop invasive breast cancer over the course of her lifetime." There are four levels of the cancer's severity and my mother was still in stage one, if she did not get treatment, she would move into stages two and three, and eventually stage four, for which the outcomes of living through are minimal. I never imagined that my mom, my rose, would become a part of those statistics.

• • •

While researching more on Breast Cancer for this story, I was given the opportunity to interview a professor at Millikin University. Professor Cindie Zelhart was diagnosed with Breast Cancer in 2003. She and her family had similar religious beliefs and experiences that my family did and their Christianity faith also kept them strong throughout her treatments and second aggressive diagnosis in 2005. She did not have many doubts about her fight and had hope and optimism of a survival outcome. "I realized God would be faithful and give me the strength I needed to get through each day. Regardless of my prognosis he's still God and worthy of my praise," Zelhart said (personal communication, April 26, 2018).

Like Zelhart and her family, my family had no doubts. We were not going to let this destroy us and tear our family apart. My mom was going to fight and she was going to win this battle. Even though we were not dwelling on the negative outcome possibilities, it was still a terrifying thought—thinking about my mom having cancer and there's always a chance, even if it's slim, that things won't go well. Just hearing my mom tell me she was sick was like an arrow to the chest and a fist crushing the roots that I had planted deep in my faith soil that I fertilized every day. I felt shattered and scared. I just couldn't understand why God would allow my mom to have cancer. It was always in the back of my mind that something could go wrong, but I tried not to think much about that because it terrified me even more to think that my mom wouldn't beat it. We all just tried to stay positive and not let this tear our family down. That's all we could do.

• • •

My parents tell me that I can go back over to my friend's house and play for another hour or two before we eat dinner. How am I supposed to go back over to my friend's house when I just found out that my mother has cancer? She's dying and I have to pretend like everything is okay. This sucks. I go to the hallway bathroom and make sure I have all of my tears wiped away, so I don't look like I have just been crying. I take a deep breath while looking at my reflection and then try to smile. If I'm not smiling and laughing with them while they're having fun, they'll ask what's wrong. I can't explain it to them yet.

I say goodbye to my parents and walk out of the house and back over to the neighbor's. They're playing video games on the GameCube, and one of the other boys who lives in the neighborhood is now over, too. They're yelling at each other about the battle game they're playing and I sit and watch their play fights without saying anything. I try to focus on the tv screen, but I can't stop thinking about my mom. What's going to happen now? Is she going to be alright? What if nothing works and she dies?

My friends ask me if I want to play a turn, and I take the controller one of them hands to me. I smile and act like everything's normal. I'm gonna have to act like everything is normal for the next six months, even though nothing is.

• • •

I played with my friends, went to church, and eventually went back to school with the news of my mom's cancer. Yet, I still couldn't say anything. I don't know if I really wanted to say anything to anyone anyways. What would that have done for me? Gained some sympathy? I didn't want anybody's pity. I just wanted my mom to live and be okay. When my parents finally told people, it was bittersweet. I was happy that we had people in our lives that surrounded my family with love and support, but it was also a constant reminder of the disease, and I wanted to forget about it. They would bring over dinners they made to last us the week and told us they were praying for us, watering the rose that was slowly wilting little-by-little.

My mom went through multiple lumpectomy surgeries to remove "only the tumor and a small amount of surrounding tissue [in the breast]" ("Lumpectomy Surgery," 2017). After the surgeries, she underwent chemotherapy and then radiation therapy. Chemotherapy is "medicines [to] prevent cancer cells from growing and spreading by destroying the cells or stopping them from dividing... Chemotherapy weakens and destroys cancer cells at the original tumor site and throughout the body" ("How Chemotherapy Works," 2016). Radiation is started after the chemotherapy and radiation therapy "uses a special kind of high-energy beam to damage cancer cells... These high-energy beams, which are invisible to the human eye, damage a cell's DNA, the material that cells use to divide" ("How Radiation Works," 2016).

I was kept in the dark some with my mother's chemo and radiation treatments. Maybe my parents didn't want me to know information, since I was so young and didn't need to know everything, but I wish I had known more about what was actually going on in her body in response to the treatments. I wanted to know why my mom was crying some of the times when she got home from work, and why she was so tired after doing the minimum of work. I did not understand, at the time, the true pain that she was feeling. How could I have known when I didn't even know what pain was? I had never felt real pain besides twisting my ankle or getting a paper cut. Those are nothing compared to a disease that slowly kills you.

Zelhart also fought relentlessly against her illness and while her faith kept her hopeful and strong, her sickness affected her husband and children. Through her first round of cancer treatments, her farmer husband was by her side and supported her through it all. Two years later when she got another diagnosis of a more aggressive tumor, her husband struggled with coping. He wanted to take care of her, but he was very angry that he could not fix this situation. Their children had a hard time grasping that she had the disease. "My son was shocked but tried not to overreact. I remember him saying breast cancer treatment has come a long way. My daughter was totally heart broken and just sobbed. I remember her saying something about she didn't want me to die," Zelhart said (personal communication, April 25, 2018).

Kate Bolick was ten years old when her mother told her she had breast cancer. As she grew up with her family, her mother's "illness became an everyday fact of [their] lives" (Bolick, 2017). Even though her mom had cancer, she did not act like she was sick. She did not give anyone doubts about her fight with this disease. This is how my family acted too. We acted like a normal family, but still in my eyes, nothing was normal anymore. I still played with my friends and went to school when the school year started up again, but it wasn't the same. I wished I could've helped. My rose was starting to wilt, and the soft petals were falling with each day that went by; I could not catch them no matter how much I tried. There was nothing that I could do to take away her pain, even though I wanted to. I didn't know what to do for her, other than be the daughter that she raised me to be. All I could do was stand back, watch and not let her fall.

My mom started to lose her hair in the first few weeks of chemo and, besides the fatigue, that was the hardest part. As more hair started to fall out, my dad would shave her head until there was nothing left. Along with the hair on her head, she also lost her eyebrows. She cried through it all, but I thought that she was still beautiful with and without hair. She was a warrior, and she became my hero for her strength and determination to fight this illness with everything she had. When Zelhart lost her hair to the chemo treatment, she wore wigs to make it appear as though she was not sick. "I didn't want to look sick, because people treat you differently when you are sick." Her children did not like seeing her without her wigs because seeing her bald head meant that her illness was real. "Neither of them wanted to see me bald. It was the only thing they didn't deal with very well," she said.

• • •

I walk into the kitchen to the aroma of my mom's food that she has been cooking for the past hour. My dad is setting the plates and silverware on the table, and I weave around my brother and the kitchen counter to grab the glasses. I set them on the table, as my mom brings the food over and places them in the middle of the placemats. We sit down and say a quick prayer over the food before we eat.

It's been six months since I was told about mom's cancer, and I think things are slowly starting to go back to normal. I'm halfway through my seventh grade year and mom has started full time at work again. I don't remember how many treatments she has left, but I think she should be done soon. I hope she is done soon.

My dad says halfway through dinner that mom just finished her last treatment today. This makes me stop eating and listen to him say that she has a checkup next week, but everything is looking good. The cancer is gone.

I want to jump up and down in excitement, but I just smile in my chair. The room now feels light and happy. I'm so happy. She's going to be okay. It's all over now.

We go back to eating and having our discussions we only ever have at the dinner table, and I am still so happy. I say a quick prayer in my head, while watching my family converse, and thank God for letting my mom live. "Thank you, God, for not taking her away."

• • •

The further away my mom got from that first day and each check up coming back without any detection of cancerous cells, life turned back to the way it was before. Only, we weren't the same family. We were stronger. But as I went through the next couple of years, there was starting to be a small question that kept coming to my mind at random times. Will I ever get cancer, too? I knew that illnesses can be hereditary or passed down; and there are greater chances of contracting the illness if an immediate family member had it first. I really tried to not ever think about that question because it scared me too much.

I didn't even want to put that thought out into the universe about how I could turn out how my mom did. I wasn't going to speak it into existence because as I got older, like Bolick stated, I believed that "my mother's fate [isn't] mine after all, genetically or sociologically" (Bolick, 2017). I am not going to torment myself with all of these negative, unnecessary thoughts. I am always staying positive and optimistic.

Looking back on that time, I now understand why I was left in the dark with some things. A child should never have to know how much their parent suffers. They need to be children and live their happy childhoods, without being tainted with pain and heartache. I still felt like a child through all this, but my mindset was still changed with what little bit of information I knew. Everyone dies and life can be extremely cruel and unfair. I learned more about life and death in this one year than I ever had before in my life. I learned about how easily something can be taken away from you, and in a blink of an eye, everything can change. Life is precious and not permanent and, at any given moment, it can be ended without your control.

Having this knowledge made me not only stronger, but it made me appreciate the life I had. My rose didn't stop growing. She fought relentlessly and beat all of the storms that came her way. She taught me how to be a strong woman who can stand on her own pedestal and fight anything that life throws at her. Life is too short to fall and submit to the negative forces that try to pin you down.

It's a lot of pressure to put on a 12-year-old girl, who never experienced real pain and heartache before, to permanently store memories of a difficult family time. I only remember bits and pieces of these six months and even these fragments that I have are blurry and vague. I can only tell this story from what I can recall at 12-years-old and try to make sense of the unclear memories in my eyes that may or may not be truly accurate. So the way I view life is going to be different than the way other people view it. Everybody has different views and everybody has their own stories to tell. Not all are the same and not all are truly accurate. We tell ourselves stories about situations we've experienced but they may not have been the real story. We forget pieces of those times or remember them so clearly they seem like they were reality. Life is about putting your pieces of memory together into your life puzzle. I've put my own pieces together of this puzzle, but there may be some pieces that are still missing. These pieces I might never find, but I am okay with that. Not everything is meant to be found and not everything is going to fit perfectly. This is only my piece of the puzzle that I have told myself is the right way to place inside. My parents have their own pieces and my brother has his own. We all live with the pieces we tell ourselves and we spend the rest of our lives telling our puzzles that only we remember in our eyes.

• • •

March 2020

Mom,

Almost ten years now since the diagnosis and nine and a half years of being cancer free. Words can't describe how proud I am of you. Thank you for showing me what a true warrior is. Your constant strength and resilience inspire me every day. I love you.

Love, your daughter,
Bekah

References

Bolick, K. (2017). Afterlives: My mother's breast cancer, and my own. *The New Yorker.* Retrieved from www.newyorker.com/books/page-turner/afterlives-my-mothers-breast-cancer-and-my-own

Breastcancer.org. (2016). *How chemotherapy works.* Retrieved from www.breastcancer.org/treatment/chemotherapy/how_it_works

Breastcancer.org. (2016). *How radiation therapy works.* Retrieved from www.breastcancer.org/treatment/radiation/how_works

Breastcancer.org. (2017). *Lumpectomy surgery for breast cancer.* Retrieved from www.breastcancer.org/treatment/surgery/lumpectomy

Breastcancer.org. (2018). *U.S. breast cancer statistics.* Retrieved from www.breastcancer.org/symptoms/understand_bc/statistics

CHAPTER 24

Piece of Me

Jelisa Lovette

Pieces of me lay about
In places where people have trodden
On sidewalks and alongside roads
Distant places that have long been 4gotten
There are pieces of me that are in places
While others you'll find outside the margin
There are pieces of me dat have been erased,
While many have been discarded, lost and never to
Be found.

Pieces of me lay in places, that are dark and
Without sound. Silently they lay on the ground
Scattered about in random places all around.
There are broken pieces of me that can't be
Assembled, pieces of me dat aren't that simple
No two pieces of me look da same,
So they never resemble,
My life is a puzzle
That lay in pieces waiting for a hand that is not
My own
So I lay here in pieces and until that hand
Arrives, I'll lay here all alone…

© KONINKLIJKE BRILL NV, LEIDEN, 2020 | DOI: 10.1163/9789004441651_025

CHAPTER 25

Nothing New under the Sun

Sandra Brown

In a class I took while incarcerated at Dwight Correctional Center nearly 20 years ago, I recall Professor Roland Johnson saying the following words: "There is nothing new under the sun." How true those words ring today in terms of what defines education and to whom access is given. Our country's history entails a time when teaching African-American slaves to read was illegal; when plowing, planting, and picking up after others comprised educating "the New Negro;" and when separate but equal set a clear yet inexplicably egregious line of demarcation between "white" and "colored" schools. Should we review our historical footprint tracking the education of women, we would surmise along with Professor Johnson that there is nothing new under the sun. Misogynistic fallacies held that women were intellectually inferior, incapable of learning academic material, and when women were first allowed to pursue education, it consisted of domestic learning. In high school, our boys learned math, science, mechanics, and engineering; our girls learned to cook, clean, and nurse babies.

"Well, we've come a long way from that," some would say. "Times have changed-everyone has access to education," others may note. I respectfully acknowledge those positions, but passionately beg to differ. What appeared to subside with the Emancipation Proclamation, Women's Suffrage, and the Civil Rights Movement has reinvented itself in the forms of Mass Incarceration, the Digital Divide, and Stand your Ground. Social Activist Susan Burton reports that the incarceration rate for women increased 700% since the 1980's; despite the fact that more than 30% were single mothers raising dependent children. In today's Information Age, women and African-Americans are twice as likely to lack computer access and quality education as white men. If those numbers aren't appalling enough to raise an eyebrow or two, then consider this: America's average incarcerated population is 2.5 million—nearly 25% of the world's prison population. According to the author and legal advocate Bryan Stevenson, approximately 100 million Americans have criminal records. And in Becoming Ms. Burton, Susan Burton reports that more than 70% of the incarcerated population cannot read above a 4th grade level. When considering the educational profile of the modern-day slave (a.k.a. prisoners), can we really refute the obvious?

Indeed, there is nothing new under the sun.

But there can be. A glaring connection exists between illiteracy and incarceration. Our historical footprint continues to travel the path of oppression was illiteracy. Though we have witnessed and experienced the transformative power of education, we continue to deny access to those who most need it because education is still perceived as a privilege and not a necessity. As an incarcerated woman, I have seen programs dwindle and disappear from female correctional facilities. What few that remain prepare women for minimum wage jobs with no benefits or full-time hours. Male correctional facilities, conversely, continue to offer college degree programs. Most incarcerated women were locked up long before we came to prison. And, were we ever asked why we remained trapped in those vicious cycles, more often than not the answer would be because we couldn't find a way out.

History has demonstrated repeatedly that knowledge is power. Education is a way out. As I tutor ABE and CoEd students who reside on the Mom's and Babies' unit in Decatur, I see how education changes their lives. I see how education changes their lives. I see how education changes how they see themselves and how that change helps their children, their families, and their communities. Children of incarcerated parents are at risk of becoming incarcerated themselves, BUT—what if that incarcerated parent had access to a college education? How much more would that decrease history's tendency to repeat itself?

I know how education has changed me. I entered Corrections a broken, empty shell of a woman who thought her life was over because she came to prison. I tried participating in educational programs but was locked out of most of them because I had a lengthy sentence and could not earn any good-time credits. Rather than grow angry and bitter with time, I grew hungry for change and pregnant with possibility.

Today, I am a doctoral student at California Coast University's Ed.D. program. Were academic college degree programs available to incarcerated women, I am undoubtedly certain that I would be one among the norm rather than one among the exceptions. Countless women over the years were inspired by my aspirations, but discouraged by the barriers commiserate with pursuing an education in prison.

This continues to be the case even today, but it doesn't have to be. Because women are often the primary caregivers of generations to come; because the recidivism rate drops drastically where prisoners have access to education; and because 96% of those incarcerated WILL return home whether they receive an education or not, it is imperative that we view education not as a privilege, but as a necessity.

One of the Ten Core Values of the Shakespeare Correctional Theatre Troupe says that how we send participants away from the community is how they come back to the community. Collectively, we can make something new under the sun. That newness requires us to bring college degree programs back into female prisons. The success and well-being of our families, communities, and society depends on it.

CHAPTER 26

Living a Life with Invisible Bars

Kathlyn J. Housh

Some things never change. Last night, I lay on the couch extremely exhausted from my day.

I thought about what it will be like when I am in heaven and no longer living this daily pain. The television was on with *Law and Order svu*. Across the room, my husband looked at Facebook on his phone. The smell of pizza flooded the room. I thought about how far I have come though still so exhausted from the constant physical ailments. My head pounded, and eyes blurred as I tried like hell to get my mind off the pain. You see, that is what they tell you in Cognitive Behavioral Therapy. You have to keep your mind off the pain. You have to distract yourself from it. Today, I am struggling to be distracted. As the head pounds, the vision blurs, the trouble putting together thoughts of anything other than how bad I feel becomes more and more difficult. Time for meditation.

• • •

The room is quiet. The lights dimmed. Anxiety runs wild through my body. The thought of where the scars will take me is overwhelming. The mental, physical and emotional scars aren't pretty, for they are many. A tear flows down my cheek. I gently touch one of my most significant scars. The deep indentation it has made, not only in my body, but also in my mind. It takes me back. I feel the gentle touch of my husband caress my hand. Unable to speak, I squeeze his hand. I hear, "she's doing it on her own. We can remove the tube." My eyes shift back to the person in the room, not knowing who they are. My husband still gently caresses my hand. My mind races with questions. The first words I utter, "Where is my baby?" My husband reassures me he is fine. I then ask, "Where am I?" Before an answer is given, I cry out in pain. My husband grabs my hand, grasping the button and helps me to push it. I fade. I continue to hear the movement around me. The smell of antiseptic causes me to open my eyes.

The nurse stands over me, gently wiping my face. Questions again fill my mind. What happened? Where am I? What day is it? My husband is still next to me, he sees the questioning look on my face. The smell of his cologne brings a smile to my face. I hear the voice of another man saying, "There is the smile

I have been waiting to see." I look over and there is a man in a dress shirt, tie, and long white coat. He introduces himself. "I am Doctor Charles. I have heard about your smile and having been waiting to see it, but it won't be here for long." He had the nurses turn me to my left side. He grabbed the chest tube attached and pulled with all his might. I scream out in absolute pain, "Ohh-hhh...Fuuuuuuccccckkkkk!" The smell of blood hits me. The room spins as I push the button again and fade.

• • •

It's about 5:30 p.m. The sun shines bright, and the smell of a light rain is in the air. I come upon the intersection where it all happened. Where my life changed forever. I travel this intersection at least twice a day if not more. However, today it is as it was "that day. The time on the clock was the time of my actual accident 17 years ago. I sit. No one is around. No traffic. The radio is playing "I can only imagine" lightly in the background. My mind starts racing trying to remember all the little details, but nothing comes. All I can think about is the pain. All of the pain that started that very day. Not only the physical pain but also the mental, emotional and spiritual pain as well. Why? Why must I endure this every day? Why, God? Why me? Still nothing comes. I must have been sitting here for 15 to 20 minutes, now unable to move. A car slowly stops behind me. Honk honk.

• • •

The alarm goes off. I roll over. The clock reads 6:30 a.m. I lay there for a few more moments thinking about the long drive ahead of us. I finally get out of bed, get ready, and head to Decatur to meet my sister, Sara. The next few days will decide what my future holds. On my way to meet her, I call my mom. She sounds happy, sad, anxious, all wrapped up in one. Her voice cracks as she tells me, "Kat, I'm praying for you. Don't give up. You have to keep fighting. You're my rock." I remember those words and play them in my mind almost daily. I told Mom that day, "If they cannot help me, I am not coming home."

• • •

Sitting alone in a Super 8. The musty smell all around me. Tears flow down my face. The question *how did I end up here?* will just not go away. The pain in my abdomen reminds me I have not left this earth yet. I am alone. I look around the room. I've never felt so alone. The phone rings, and I pick up the receiver. A raspy voice on the other end says, "Your shuttle is here." I grab my coat and run out the door, down the stairs. I climb on to the shuttle and grab a seat at the back by myself. I am not in the mood to talk to anyone or even pretend to be nice. Left turn. Right turn. Stop. Go. Snow continually falling. After what seems like an eternity, we finally arrive. I have never been so scared and so alone. The pain radiates through my body reminding me of why I am here.

• • •

Alone in the room, there is nothing familiar to me other than the constant pain from which I can never seem to find relief. When I checked in, they took *all* of my prescription medications. These pills are how I function. These meds are now me. They are who I have become. The anger I felt was undeniable. I said a few choice words to the nurse. There is no way she could understand! There is absolutely no familiarity. I had no one. I sat among complete strangers. The room is small with approximately 15 of us crammed in. There are a couple of small windows, but otherwise the room is dull and bare. I thought to myself *what did you expect? It is a hospital setting!* This "older" woman stands in front of the "class" talking about our homework we need to have done by tomorrow. She instructs us on how to create our timeline of critical events in our lives and gives an example. We are to note the first time we ever took a drink of alcohol, as it related to this timeline. The same with pain medicines. We are to note if any of our family members have addictions. Note this... Note that... "Create your timeline." I think to myself, "Screw this." Then suddenly my mind goes back to the words of my mom, "Don't give up. You are my rock."

I asked the woman in the front of the class, "how is this supposed to help me?" Her answer: "Do you have a family history of addiction? Do you take more pain medicines than prescribed? Do you take them when you are not in pain? Why do you take them?" Question after question. I look around the room again. Tears flowing down the faces of these complete strangers. The woman in the front says, "You are free to go for the day." I head back to my hotel and begin my timeline. 1993, first drink of alcohol. 1994, birth of first son by C-section (pain pills given). 1995, first car accident (pain pills given). 1996, wrist surgery for broken wrist (pain pills given). 1999, birth of second son by C-section (pain pills given). 2000, second car accident (pain pills given). It hits me sitting right there alone in a hotel room hundreds of miles away from everyone I love and need in my life. "I have been on pain pills on and off since 1994. Then, since that fateful day in March of 2000, pain pills non-stop, sometimes up to 12 a day. I have sweat pouring from my body. My heart is racing. My nose is running. I am shaking and just cannot stop. All I can think is, "what the hell?" I pick up the phone and dial my nurse's number at Mayo. He informs me that I need to come in right away. I hang up the phone, grab my coat and run down to catch the shuttle.

I arrive at Mayo's Pain Rehab Clinic in about 10 minutes. My nurse checks all of my vitals and says I am experiencing some withdrawals. He goes on to say "it will get worse before it gets better, but that is why you are here. Mayo's Pain Rehab Clinic (PRC) is going to help you learn how to manage your pain without the need for all of the medications. Doctor Loftus referred you here for Cognitive Behavioural Therapy (CBT)." According to Mayo

Clinic, CBT is a common type of talk therapy also known as psychotherapy (Mayo Clinic, 2017). CBT helps you to develop strategies for coping with pain and avoiding high-risk addictive pain medications.

According to the *Journal of Psychiatric Practice*, opioids are commonly prescribed to treat pain. However, CBT is used to teach patients a different way to deal with chronic pain and is an effective way to drive down the unnecessary use of opioid prescriptions (Toich, 2017). Before coming to Mayo Clinic, I had no idea I could deal with the daily pain from over 15 abdominal surgeries and 3 major motor vehicle accidents without the use of prescription pain medications. Research provides evidence supporting the use of CBT for substance abuse disorders and pain management, including a variety of interventions that emphasize different targets. One of the most important targets is your motivation for treatment. Motivation—*my* motivation was, and continues to be, my "baby." I guess I shouldn't call him my baby anymore. He is 19. I had no idea what CBT even was until I went to Mayo. All I knew is that I needed help. I was tired of living in pain. It didn't even click with me that I was an "addict" until my time I spent at PRC. The timeline was the real revelation for me, along with sitting in a room with 14 other "addicts." I could relate with so many of them.

They ALL were dealing with their pain the same way I was, through prescription pain pills.

• • •

I look out the window of my hotel room. The snow is really coming down. The smell of chlorine fills the room. I say to myself, "it must be time to treat the pool and hot tub again." I have become used to talking to myself. The phone rings. "Hello." "Hey, Kat. It's Mom."

Terri and I are downstairs." The waterworks start. I go running down the stairs. I don't want to wait for the elevator. I see my mom. I cannot believe she and Terri (my best friend) drove hundreds of miles to come see me. I cannot let go of my momma's neck. She cried. I cried. Terri cried. "We are here until Sunday." I jumped for joy! The snow still comes down. It looks like a blizzard out there. We grab the elevator and head back to my room. Mom and Terri get unpacked. I make some coffee even though it is close to 11:00 p.m. None of us can sleep anyway. We sit up until 2 a.m. just talking. I shared with my mom for the first time that I am an addict. It was something I was able to hide for years. My family and close friends had seen me take "pills" before, but never knew just what it was or how much I actually took. The tears were falling profusely down my mom's slightly wrinkled face. I tell her how sorry I am for failing her and allowing myself to let the pain take over my life. Momma's words, "Kathy, you have nothing to be sorry for. You chose to come here and get better. I am proud of you." To hear the words, that she is still proud of me, allows me to close my eyes and sleep the best I had in a very long time.

• • •

The sun shines so bright and the smell of coffee floods the room. It is a new day. The day I am going home. The anticipation of seeing my husband and son overwhelms me. The fear starts to take over. I start to wonder… What are they going to think? What are they going to say? Are they going to look at me different now? I start to break out in a sweat with this drowning fear. I sip from my coffee cup, as I continue to pack my belongings. I recall how I could have left Mayo PRC (Pain Rehab Clinic) at any time, but my motivation was my family. I had to get better. I could not continue on the road I was on. The sun shines a little brighter, and a gentle smile comes across my face. The phone rings and I pick it up. "Kat, it's Mom. Are you ready to come home?" "Heck yes, Mom!" I share with her my fears. She now understands after herself being "schooled" from my team of doctors. The words stick with me today like never before, "Kat, he doesn't see you as an addict. He refuses to believe that. You're his mom."

Mom begins to share with me about how when she got back home from visiting me she called a "family meeting." My husband, youngest son, sister and daughter-in-law were all there. My oldest son was in basic training during this time. Although, the mom he knew when he left is not the Mom he will see when he graduates. My Mom went into every detail from what she had learned with them and even had them watch the DVD about chronic pain and opiate addiction. Mom said, "Briley refused." She said his words were, "that is NOT my mom. She is my mom and she is strong, and that is not who she is." I guess he then departed to his "man cave" at their house. To this day, he refuses to believe or even discuss the struggle I have. He just always says, "that is not who you are,

Mom." I love the fact that he sees me for me, not for my addiction. He sees the person and not the label society gave me!

• • •

"Ms. Housh, we need to give you a prescription for Tylenol with Codeine. This will help suppress your cough you've had for months and will also allow you to get some sleep," the doctor's voice fades out as fear overtakes my body. Sweat breaks out on my forehead. My hands are clammy. My mind races with question after question. Do I tell him I have a history of addiction? Does he already know? Will this send me back into relapse? What do I do? I feel the sweat pouring down my armpits. However, the uncontrollable coughing breaks the silence. As I try to speak through the coughing, I hear him say "only for a short-time..." Three days. Three days is all it took for me to say "NO." I stopped the narcotic. I do not NEED it.

• • •

The realization I am an addict is a scary one. It took a very long time to come to it. However, it is *not* who I am. It is *not* my identity. It is the label society gave me. Being a recovering addict is just a small part of my journey. Just as it took me a long time to realize I am an addict, it took me until just recently to realize that is not who I am. My son has known it the entire time and now I know it. I believe we all are given a journey to walk in this life. Because of my journey, I built up walls. The walls built over the years from past mistakes, past hurts and past failures, especially the label given "addict." If you were to ask me today who I am, my answer would not include the label of a recovering addict. I am a wife, a mother, a daughter, a sister, a friend, I am me! I am proud of the person I am today. I have peeled away the layers and allowed God to tear down the walls. Because of this, I am a stronger survivor. My scars do not define me. My addiction does not define me. In the words of *Mandisa*, I am an OVERCOMER. I leave you with the chorus of her song that I continue to cling to during my most difficult days:

> ... You're an overcomer
> Stay in the fight 'til the final round
> You're not going under
> 'Cause God is holding you right now
> You might be down for a moment

Feeling like it's hopeless
That's when he reminds you
That you're an overcomer
You're an overcomer.
(Mandisa, 2013, Single)

My struggle with pain and opioid addiction are my prison. However, I choose daily to overcome and not let these invisible bars define my life.

References

Mandisa. (2013). *Overcomer* [CD]. Brentwood: Chuck Butler, David Garcia, Ron Rawls, Christopher Stevens.

McHugh, R., Hearon, K., Bridget, A., & Otto, M. W. (2010). Cognitive-behavioral therapy for substance use disorders. *Psychiatric Clinic North America, 33*(3), 511–525.

Nash, R. R., Ponto, J., Townsend, C., Nelson, P., & Bretz, M. N. (2013). Cognitive behavioural therapy, self-efficacy, and depression in persons with chronic pain. *Pain Management Nursing, 14*(4), 236–243. doi:10.1016/j.pmn.2012.02.006

CHAPTER 27

Where Would I Be

Jelisa Lovette

Where would I be
If my Lord & Savior would never thought to create thee
Where would I be
If my mom wouldn't have mistakenly conceived me
Where would I be
If she decided to abort me, where would I be?
Somewhere flushed down a drain
Somewhere buried with little or evaporated remains.
Now that I think about it, who would I blame?
I guess nobody because I'm here right,
But that still doesn't stop my mind from wondering at night.
Just wondering, where would I really be?
If I wouldn't have given the haters and the women
every inch of my energy
Where would I be?
If I hadn't of taken my wins with my losses
being able to separate do real from da fake, you never
know what you gone get wit these women's personalities, be able
to pick heads or tails, flip em' like coin tosses.
Where would I be?
If death was never a part of the equation,
If convincing wasn't da same thing as persuasion
If my mind could take over da feelings in my heart
on every lusting occasion and prevent a love invasion.
Where would I be?
Hurt, broken hearted, depressed, angry, sad,
but where would dat get me?
Damage, pain, negativity, fire, red is all I'll be able to see.
but right now I'll take all dat and put it towards my GED
because while I'm here as a prisoner with invisible
chains, it's the only thing I feel will set me free.
Where would I be?
Sometimes I feel like I'm that mockingbird to kill,

© KONINKLIJKE BRILL NV, LEIDEN, 2020 | DOI: 10.1163/9789004441651_028

being held against my will and like dat mocking-
bird I'm stuck at a stand still
But I'll rise, spread my beautiful wings and fly
No longer be a caged bird, I'll no longer allow
my eyes to cry.
No longer allow my heart to bleed
No longer choose my wants before my need
Knowing that I'm a different type of breed
Always hungry but before I eat, I feed.
I'm that nicely moisten soil, that covers the seed,
It'll take years to grow, but even then, still
Where would I be?

CHAPTER 28

My Odyssey

Sandra Brown

Her name is Calypso,
the goddess giving me
this Odyssian experience.
She holds hope hostage,
weaning my mind
of memories
like babies
from Momma's milk.

Year after year,
she skillfully
siphons away
facets of freedom
and tucks it away
on Ogygian.
A little here—
(don't think about that now),
A little there—
(that part of your life is over).
When I realize
what she's doing
and rebel,
she hides my dreams
in the mountains
and valleys
of Here and Now.

You thought because Time
temporarily befriended you
that Love would die
without a trace,
and R35900

© KONINKLIJKE BRILL NV, LEIDEN, 2020 | DOI: 10.1163/9789004441651_029

would be the death
of my dreams.

But Time waits for no one.
Not even you.

You've persuaded Time
to put lives on lockdown,
but iron,
barbed wires
and bricks
just aren't strong enough
to hold a Dream
destined to be.

CHAPTER 29

What Makes Straight so Great?

Dwight G. Brown, Jr.

I don't know who I am. Why? Because, I've spent most of my life making decisions based on the pleasure of others, as most African Americans do. As an African American male, the bad decisions you make go mainstream, while the good decisions rarely get noticed.

Compared to white men and women, African Americans must be more careful, because, for us, one slip up can be our last; there are few things that protect us. In my last paper, published in the third volume of this series, I described the extreme caution we, as a race, take as "walking on eggshells." And that's exactly what we've been doing. Most people don't understand what "walking on eggshells" means for all black men and women. Walking on eggshells for us means changing how we speak.

Walking on eggshells for us means changing how we look. Walking on eggshells for us means being someone we aren't. We do this regardless of the consequences, because, since slavery days, all we've yearned for is acceptance. We sacrifice dignity, we sacrifice integrity, we sacrifice loyalty all to be accepted by a society that won't accept us regardless. This paper revolves around one aspect of "walking on eggshells" and that part is changing how we look. I've walked on eggshells for a number of reasons and I've done it in a number of ways. This time walking on eggshells meant cutting my dreads. I chose to cut my dreads for many reasons, the most evident of these was perception. How will I be perceived without dreadlocks and how I am perceived with them? In exploring how much the perception of people with dreadlocks matters, I approached this essay from a workplace standpoint. Having a job is one of the essential requirements for living in today's society. So what does dreadlocks mean to the work world?

• • •

For a very long time now, dreadlocks—or "locs"—as a hairstyle, have been looked down upon. What people don't seem to realize is that for African Americans, along with other races, dreadlocks are not only a natural hairstyle, but a mark of culture. Dreadlocks aren't new. They date back as far as 2500 B.C., with just about every civilization in history having worn them at one time. Ancient

Egyptian Pharaohs wore locs, as seen on ancient carvings. Religious figures, such as Samson from the old testament and the Hindu God Shiva, also wore locs. So locs are anything but recent and unnatural. Back then, there weren't any hair products, so people had no choice but to twist and style their hair as is. The only way dreadlocks become unnatural is when someone who doesn't have the proper hair texture (white people) attempt to get dreads. Society puts dreadlocks down, and has taken the identity of dreadlocks and twisted it. The color of the person wearing the dreadlocks is also a very important factor when it comes to their acceptance. Thinking back to when we see color determining the acceptance of dreads is when Giuliana Rancic referred to singer/actor Zendaya's locs as smelling like "weed and oil," while she referred to Kylie Jenner's dreadlocks as "edgy." To make matters worse, after a case involving a woman of color with dreadlocks in the workplace, the United States Court made an unbelievable decision. In 2016, the United States Court ruled that not hiring someone for having dreadlocks is completely legal.

According to Rushay Booysen, NBC web writer, not hiring someone for having dreadlocks is legal, because regardless of culture ties, if it's changeable, you're not protected by law (Gutierrez-Morfin, 2016). Dreadlocks already had negative associations with them outside of the workplace, so to see these discriminations in the workplace wasn't too shocking. If you were someone with dreadlocks, you simply did what you had to do. I had dreadlocks, and, "of my own will," I cut them, because my mind was corrupt. I began to believe what society was saying: "Dreadlocks aren't professional." My long term goal is to be an actor and, part of the reason I cut my dreadlocks, is because I do not want to be type- casted. Should I choose to keep my dreads, how will I be portrayed? Will I only be seen as a thug? This is just how society sees most people who have dreadlocks. This is what I had accepted. I have not been turned down from a job for my dreadlocks, but part of me believes that this is only because I cut them before I interviewed for a professional job.

What I have gotten are looks, matter of fact, piercing stares. It's like when you know people are staring into you, opposed to "at" you. This piercing stare has changed since I've cut my dreadlocks. It is now a positive look, rather than a stare.

The sad thing about it is, I'm the same me, with different hair.

• • •

So, can dreadlocks actually reduce your chances of obtaining a job? This is way more than a hairstyle question. Due to the fact that "locs" are more than a hairstyle, this question not only touches on workplace expectations, but personal expression and cultural sensitivity, as well. To answer the question above, after analyzing several interviews with people with dreads, we see that in a white collar world, dreadlocks put you at a high disadvantage.

These interviews also show that when it comes to having dreadlocks, and, whether or not it will be accepted, depends on where you are. Through researching this topic, I came across a few interviews that contradict each other. When interviewed by Phillip Walzer, writer for the *Virginian Pilot*, in 2014, Kisha Brown, owner of a Dreadlocks salon in Portsmouth Virginia, says she's seen all kinds of clients in her store. The Virginian Pilot is a local newspaper of Norfolk Virginia, which is not too far from where both interviewees below live. According to Walzer, Kisha says she has seen White, Asian, and African Americans in her store. Her clients' professions ranged from Attorneys to Store Managers. Kisha believes that, in Virginia, dreadlocks don't affect your hireability. Kisha says, "I've watched people go up the corporate ladder with dreadlocks. It seems that most Virginia employers are not looking at them as such a bad thing anymore." The interesting thing about Kisha's statement is that during that same year, Hampton University, a school located in Virginia, was prohibiting males with locks and cornrows from attending a seminar in its combined five-year bachelor's-master's program in business. How are those with either of these hairstyles affected? Well, it comes down to two choices. You can fight it or accept it.

Also interviewed by Walzer (2014), Tyler Bailey was an athlete at the time who chose to accept that society has negative associations towards dreads. So much so that it could deny you a job. Tyler says, "I was playing football. I liked the way I looked." Although he enjoyed the way his hair looked, in the end, he still cut it. Since cutting his dreads, he's graduated with a Law degree from Southern University's law school in Louisiana. Both are things that could have been done with or without dreadlocks. Don't misalign dreadlocks with levels of intelligence. After receiving his degree, Bailey said he appreciates what Hampton University was trying to do. Bailey appreciating Hampton University doesn't take away from the problem, which is something he also acknowledges. He knew with the career field he was choosing, dreadlocks would narrow his job prospects: "It's not accepted in certain circles in white-collar corporate America. It's unfortunate, but that's the way it is."

These two stories succeed when it comes down to showing how easy it is for African Americans to accept what people say you should look like. Tyler and Kisha understood the stereotypes having dreadlocks brought on, and, instead of challenging them, they accepted them. Tyler cut his dreads while Kisha experienced denial. She ignored the stories like Tyler's that occurred in Virginia and conjured up her own opinions. I believe that this was partially because she was the owner of a hair salon. While she didn't say it, you can concur that, since she styled the heads of different races, if it had gotten out that she believed dreadlocks had any negative associations, she'd most likely lose customers.

Not all are so accepting of society's ideals. In and out of the workplace, women have been fighting for more than just equality. Although there are acts, laws, and organizations that reinforce these, workplace discrimination continuously occurs. Not everyone is protected from these laws. Especially people of color.

• • •

The U.S. Equal Employment Opportunity Commission (EEOC) is one of the organizations that reinforces the laws to make sure all people are protected from discrimination in the workplace. If EEOC feels as though you've been discriminated against, because of race, color, religion, sex (including pregnancy, gender identity, and sexual orientation), national origin, age (40 or older), disability or genetic information, they will investigate. Upon further investigation, if evidence supports that discrimination has occurred, they have the authority to file a lawsuit to protect an individual's rights.

Chastity Jones is the case that brought hair discrimination regarding dreadlocks to light. In 2016, EEOC filed a lawsuit on behalf of Mrs. Chastity Jones against Catastrophe Management Solutions (CMS). Chastity Jones was a black woman whose employment was rejected after being hired. Yes. You heard that right. Chastity was hired by Catastrophe Management (CMS), meaning she went through the interview process, and was accepted as a candidate to only later be fired by CMS.

Catastrophe Management Solutions (CMS) is a processing company in Mobile, Alabama that provides customer service to insurance companies. In 2010, CMS announced their interest in potential employee candidates. With this information, Mrs. Jones seized the opportunity to apply. A few days later, Chastity was selected for an in person interview, to which she wore a blue dress suit and her hair in short dreads. Mrs. Jones, along with other candidates chosen, were brought into a room by CMS Human Resources Manager Jeannie Wilson. After bringing them into the room, Mrs Wilson informed them that they had been hired and that there are additional requirements that they would have to complete. Mrs. Wilson also informed candidates on what they're to do if they had scheduling conflicts. Mrs. Jones had a conflict with the lab test and she was told by Mrs. Wilson that she could return another day for the lab test. Once the conversation ended, before Mrs. Jones left, Mrs. Wilson asked if Mrs.

Jones had dreadlocks in her hair, which she did. To Mrs. Jones' answer, Mrs Wilson replied that CMS could not hire her with dreadlocks.

As surprising as this was, Mrs. Jones asked why? To which Mrs. Wilson's reply then was "they tend to get messy, although I'm not saying yours are, but you know what im talking about" (2010, Wilson, Jeannie). What made this encounter discriminatory is the fact that CMS, at the time, actually had a race grooming policy. The policy stated that "All personnel are expected to be dressed and groomed in a manner that projects a professional and business like image, while adhering to company and industry standards and/or guidelines. Hairstyle should reflect a business/professional image. No excessive hairstyles or unusual colors are acceptable."

Chastity's hair was of natural color and not messy, as Mrs. Wilson pointed out. If it's not messy, it's of natural color, and short, how does this hairstyle go against CMS policy? The problem lies not in the hairstyle. The problem lies not in the race. The problem lies in both the hairstyle and the race. Chastity didn't get hired because she was black with dreads. Chastity just wanted to work for an organization associated with mostly white people. But to do this, she had to first conform to their standards. Some of these standards were written, while others weren't. What's unprofessional about this woman's hair?

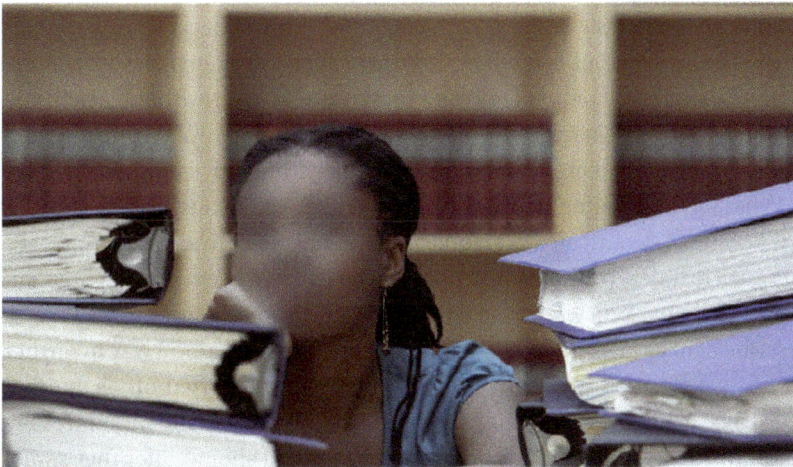

To this question there is only one right answer. The only problem with this woman's look is that it doesn't meet some standard that's been set for only a certain type of person or people. Another thing about this woman's look is that she has the face of a tired and fed up black woman. All women already face a beauty standard, so, to go to work and have to meet another standard, makes things harder on African American women. When it comes to standards you need to think about two things. The first is, who set the standard. The second is, for whom is the standard "really" set.

• • •

African Americans often have to decide how to wear their hair based on what's socially acceptable. If it is long, we have to ask "should I perm it to make it straight or just always wear it up, or do I need to do all of the above? If I have dreadlocks and want to work for a fortune 500 company, should I cut them off? Which is the most socially accepted?" As African Americans, we already are at a disadvantage with race alone, so the pressure is on with us. We are forced into the corner. By this, I mean we do whatever we can to take away from the fact that we are black. Apparently "Black is bad." These alterations consist of things like cutting hair, perming hair straight, changing the way we speak, discrediting where we come from, and doing plastic surgery. Sometimes we go as far as dying our skin. As I said earlier, we do this to be more accepted by society. Not all workplaces admit to discrimination and making people alter themselves, as we saw in the Chastity Jones case, with Mrs. Wilson's ridiculous reason as to why her dreads aren't accepted.

While hair may seem like a small alteration, it is a gateway to more severe alterations. Some people will argue that not being hired because of your hair is not discrimination, but it is when there are several discrepancies within the hiring decision. Some companies even sugar coat this and say that black is neither bad nor good; "it's just not the right fit for us as a company." Within jobs and schools, we face the debate of nappy vs. natural, with nappy being a subjective term. What straight haired people or most (White Americans) call "NAPPY" is what we (African Americans) or people without naturally straight hair, call natural. The correct description would honestly be extremely curly or slightly tangled. If you look back on where the term originated from, it started out as a term to "describe a fuzzy layer of yarn or cloth, but later on, it became a way to further insult African slaves" (Ariane, 2017). The word "NAPPY" started off as another "N" word. So dreadlocks not being accepted could have actually been foreseen based on this knowledge. Regardless, just because you should infer that something will happen, it doesn't determine the ethics behind that something. This is not "you should have seen this coming." This is more like, IT SHOULDN'T STILL BE HAPPENING. If looked at from the view of non-socially desirable attributes, one would be able to see that our natural isn't accepted (dreadlocks), while other races natural is. This is from where the problem originates

With what I've just presented to you, it is clear that people who do not have the desired look based on society's standards are forced to make alterations to fit them. Should they choose not to, their life is negatively affected. Consisting of things like not being considered for hire. This is not a NEW problem, it's an ONGOING problem. I close the essay with one simple question: What is an oppressor? Someone that stops you from being your best self. This is my definition of an oppressor. Being told who you should be. This is my definition of oppressed. We can't put all the blame on the oppressor. As the oppressed, there are things we should and shouldn't do if we want to make things right. What we shouldn't do is allow our youth to use the term "nappy" freely. We should start with them and educate them on how hurtful that term can be and where it comes from. To use it when teasing someone who looks just like you only gives power to those oppressing people with "NAPPY" hair. We can't bring one another down, but fight so that others won't. We shouldn't make songs with the lyrics "skinny jeans on and you know my hair nappy" (Juju on That Beat, McCall & Hilfigerr). Depending on how this song is taken, it could either enable people to reinforce this term (straight haired) or make people more comfortable with how they wear their hair. We must be careful what we do. If only everyone had to be this careful. African Americans can't go around or jump over the eggshells. No. No matter what we do we must walk on those eggshells.

References

Ariane. (2017, December 30). *This history of the word nappy and its naughty roots.* Black NAPS (Natural & Proud Sistas). Retrieved from https://blacknaps.org/is-nappy-a-bad-word/

Finley, T. (2016, September 20). Appeals court rules employers can ban dreadlocks at work. *HuffPost.* Retrieved from https://www.huffingtonpost.com/entry/appeals-court-rules-dreadlocks-work_us_57e0252ae4b0071a6e08a7c3

Gabbara, P. (2016, October 16). The history of dreadlocks. *Ebony.* Retrieved from http://www.ebony.com/style/history-dreadlocks

Gutierrez-Morfin, N. (2016, September 21). U.S. court rules dreadlock ban during hiring process is legal. *NBC News.* Retrieved from https://www.nbcnews.com/news/nbcblk/u-s-court-rules-dreadlock-ban-during-hiring-proces-legal-n652211

United States District Court for the Southern District of Alabama. (2016). *Equal employment opportunity commission v. catastrophe management solutions* (pp. 2–6). United States District Court for the Southern District of Alabama.

Walzer, P. (2014, August 10). Will dreadlocks keep you from getting a job? Depend. *The Virginian Pilot.* Retrieved from https://pilotonline.com/business/jobs/article_56f0d89f-14e4-5ff2-a33a-1d482f28b998.html

CHAPTER 30

Nature's Sanctuary

Angie Oakes

Trees gently swaying in the wind.
The smell of honeysuckle and wild
flowers fill my nose.

If I listen really careful I can hear
a woodpecker pecking in the
distance. I can feel the grass under
my feet as I walk.

Nature's noises are my corrected
silence. I come to a spot where I can feel
the sun on my face.

It's like being embraced by a lover: warm
and inviting.

Right here in this moment, my heart is
full of peace and tranquility.

This is where I am when my eyes close.
Having to open them is like
sinking in quicksand.

Once open, I'm back in the
present moment, in prison.

© KONINKLIJKE BRILL NV, LEIDEN, 2020 | DOI: 10.1163/9789004441651_031

CHAPTER 31

Nature's Pride and Promise

Cara Quiett

So many tragedies
on the Sunniest of days.
Bones shatter beneath the billowy
bonnets of clouds peaceful enough
to cradle an angel.
While ants march through sappy
blood streaming through blades
of luscious grass.
The music to the fallen heroes
and villains alike
is the joyful chirping of birds.
Are they mocking their terror?
Or singing them off to meet
their makers?
Those acrobats, teetering
the tightrope between life and death,
do they count the twinkling stars above
as the tears interrupt their vision?
Or count those last labored breaths?
Adventurers dedicate their lives to
conquer glorious mountains that
simply. Be.
They don't need anything but are
a deadly feat to endure.
All the while, you could admire
them from afar.
These steep, jagged sirens
of nature that call upon you
to explore her at the cost of life.
Babies cry out in the darkest
of caves while entire cities

© KONINKLIJKE BRILL NV, LEIDEN, 2020 | DOI: 10.1163/9789004441651_032

are long forgotten.
A snowflake floats gently
on frozen flesh and
somewhere there is a
rainbow in the distance.

CHAPTER 32

Finding Stability in Motion

Megan Batty

Reflection

For fourteen years, I have called myself a dancer. It has been the first thing I say when I am asked to describe myself or asked what I do. It has been my identifier for the majority of my life. The moment I decided I wanted to take dance classes was the moment my life truly changed. If I had never experienced that moment, my life would not have turned out how it has. I would have gone down a much different path, one that was not as straight and narrow.

My parents' divorce would have caused me more anxiety and trust issues if I was not able to go to dance class every week, shut off my brain, and learn how to express my emotions in a healthy way. In his article The Impact of Divorce on Young Children and Adolescents, Carl E. Pickhardt states, "For the young child, divorce shakes trust in dependency on parents who now behave in an extremely undependable way" (Pickhardt, 2011).

I also probably would not have been able to handle my father's deployments as well as I did if I did not have my studio to turn to or the therapeutic outlet that dance became for me. I more than likely would have developed behavioural problems or my grades would have declined, like my brother's, if I did not have dance. Trenton James and Jacqueline Countryman state, "More recent findings with deployed service members with children have shown problems with sleeping, higher stress levels and anxiety, declining grades, an increase in maladaptive child behaviors" (James, 2012). While I did experience stress and anxiety during these events, my life still stayed somewhat stable. I attribute that to dance. I had an outlet for these concerns, fears, and hardships, whereas my brother did not and he did experience behavioral problems, trust issues, and declining grades. I believe if he had had an outlet or a coping mechanism like I had with my dancing, our lives would not have veered off so much from each other.

I cannot imagine my life without dance. It has been my biggest impactor and teacher. Not only has it helped me get through some of my toughest times and lowest points, but it has also helped me discover who I am. I believe that everyone should have an outlet to express themselves through and to help them deal with the stressors in their lives. Dance has become my coping mechanism for

© KONINKLIJKE BRILL NV, LEIDEN, 2020 | DOI: 10.1163/9789004441651_033

all of my troubles and it has become the outlet for me to comfortably express
myself.

PART ONE
A girl.
Only seven.
Small.
Lost.
Staring through
The glass door at the
Girl whom she calls
Her best friend.
A long, billowing skirt trailing
Behind
Her as she glides across the floor
And leaps through the air.
What is remembered, though, Is not
the dance her friend performed.
But the smile which engulfed her face.
It was pure happiness.
It was pure joy.
The little girl wanted that.
She wanted to feel
The same happiness, The
same joy. She
needed Happiness.
She needed Joy.
She needed a place to call her
home. She needed a distraction. Her
family was no longer Whole.
She was shuttled
from One house To
another.
Back
And
Forth.
Again, and again.
She was only seven.
She was being put in
Between

Her fighting parents
And instead of being able
To revert to a more childish state of mind (Pickhardt, 2011),
She was forced to grow up.
She did not know it at the time,
But she was starting
To close herself off.
She needed happiness.
She needed joy.
She needed something
That would always be there.
Something, someplace
She could
Always
Run to when she needed
Solace.
Peace.
Comfort.
A home.
Looking through that glass door,
At the little girl
Whom she loved like a sister,
At the little girl
Who was having so much fun.
At the little girl who was dancing.
She decided, then and there, she wanted
To do that too.
She wanted to dance.
So she did.

PART TWO
The first time my dad left,
I had to leave my home too.
My grandmother became my caregiver.
My guardian.
My dance mom.
My father was in Iraq.
My mother was in another state.

I was nine when he left.

I was almost ten when he came
Back.

I was one of more than two million children
Worrying about their parent (James, 2012).
Waiting on weekly phone calls.
Watching for an email to find its way
Into my inbox.
Hoping that the soldiers who died in roadside bombings
Did not share my last name.

I had to take on the responsibility of being Older
than I was (2018).
Of being a "mother" figure for my little brother.
I became stressed (James, 2012).
My brother's grades started to decline (James, 2012).
For fifteen months, I almost forgot what it meant
To be a
Nine
Year
Old
Girl.

Even though my dad was an ocean away,
My grandmother took pride in taking me to dance.
Watching me perform in her living room.
Sitting through my recital costume fashion shows.
Nursing my bumps and bruises I acquired When I fell.
And picking me back up.

I latched on to the only constant I had left.
Dance.
I developed a newfound love and
Passion for this art form
That would help me deal with
Worry and panic (2018).
And the loneliness and sadness that
crashed Down like a wave over me Each
time my dad was deployed (2018).
This sport allowed to me still feel loved

And wanted, even when neither of my parents
Were around.

I found an outlet for my many new stressors (James, 2012).
I found a place where I could vent my worries
Without saying them out loud.
At nine years old, I found a life line to hold
Onto when it seemed the rest of my world was
Going to crumble at any moment.

Dance became my home.
My therapy.
My only source of hope.
It became my dream.

PART THREE
—two seconds in,
four seconds out—

The blinding white light produces sweat even from fifty feet away
The music engulfing me reverberates through my bones.

Four unnoticeably shaky steps downstage.

—two seconds in,
four seconds out—

As I start to move, my muscles loosen and take me along
A path they know all too well.
As the notes to Hallelujah guide my limbs through
Their contractions and grandiose turns,
My mind disappears into a comfortable solitude Encased by the spotlight.
And I soar across the stage.

I am lost.

Sadly, I still find my way and reach my final destination
All too soon.
The light fades, causing my skin prickle and bump.
The only sound is the pounding in my chest—at least for a moment—

The air erupts into a thunderous roar
And I realize my lungs are screaming right along with it.

—two seconds in,
four seconds out—

I feel the wetness flow down my cheeks as I walk off
For the very last time.

—two seconds in,
four seconds out—

References

James, T., & Countryman, J. (2012, February). *Psychiatric effects of military deployment on children and families: The use of play therapy for assessment and treatment.* National Institutes of Health. Retrieved from https://www.ncbi.nlm.nih.gov/pmc/articles/PMC3312898/

Military.com. (2018). *How deployment stress affects families.* Retrieved from https://www.military.com/deployment/effects-deployment-families.html

Pickhardt, C. (2011, December 19). The impact of divorce on young children and adolescents. *Psychology Today.* Retrieved from https://www.psychologytoday.com/blog/surviving-your-childs adolescence/201112/the-impact-divorce-young-children-and-adolescents

CHAPTER 33

Queen of Soul

Jelisa Lovette

Her name is Aretha, Aretha Franklin to be exact.

She spoke for us through her music, she was our voice—she had our backs. She was named the Queen of Soul, the only Queen I've ever seen with a pink Cadillac.

On her "Freeway of Love," she rode her way and made history turning her pain into inspiring music. I'm honored to use my poetry to tell some of her story.

Aretha understood how hard times was something all blacks went through and I can relate, still to this day we're here living proof every single day thanking our heavenly father as we "Say a Little Prayer" for those who were taught differently, too.

They could not help it, they were raised to hate, so they are not to blame, but we all bleed blood, we all shed tears, we are all equal, which makes us all one in the same.

It's our voices that are black so beautiful, with an image that we will forever maintain.

"R-E-S-P-E-C-T," I found out exactly what it meant to me, what it meant for me to be free.

A year ago, you would not even thought I was trying to get my G.E.D., but it was women like this Queen of Soul who truly inspired me.

And now I'm going after my masters in psychology.

Aretha Franklin was more than a daughter, a mother, a sister, she was "our" voice next to our civil rights activist.

She taught for us through her music, giving Otis Redding's original song an all-around feminist twist.

We have all been a "Chain of Fools" but that "Natural Woman" still exists.

We all just have to find our voices, "Think" and make the right choices.

As women we could run the world, all we need is unity, you see the men stick together like juice on jerry curls, so in honor of Aretha, this is my eulogy.

Aretha made music that without a doubt touched people's soul, especially women. She let it be known that no matter what we all have been through, we are that "Rose who is still and always will be a Rose." She left us too soon, God took the good too young. Aretha Franklin fought for greatness; she knew just what "we" as a united nation could really become.

She was what my grandpa would call "a smoking gun." So, with that, here's some of her story told, rest in paradise our history's only Beautiful Black Queen of Soul.

CHAPTER 34

Melodies & Recipes

Cara Quiett

The very first chef to ever capture my attention was Swedish Chef from The Muppets. I would attempt to impersonate his squinted eyes and phoney European accent. I got a kick out of the way he would playfully toss food around while delivering his famous one liner, "Poot de fish in de pot!"

From there, PBS introduced me to Julia Child. I assumed her kitchen smelled like my great grandmother's. My Gommy's kitchen smelled of flour, spices, and moth balls. It was not until I became much older that I realized what these smells actually were. But to me, I associated them with comfort.

Julia Child lured me in with her distinguishing, soothing voice. It's very jolly and sing-songy. Most people around thirty-three or older should be able to pick her voice out of a line up. She also had my favorite kind of arms. Once again, reminding me of my great grandmother. She didn't have the swoll, toned, elegant arms most people admire in magazines. Julia had regular, wonderfully flabby old lady arms. The type best for embracing.

I would stare at our old television while willing Julia to stop her kneading and striving to walk through the screen and hug me. Of course this would never happen, but I would hug myself and imagine that it was her.

My interest in cooking shows, chefs, and food started at a young age. I was experimenting with recipes long before I could reach the counter or stove. During high school I was the only teacher's aid for home economics to avoid gym, my least favorite class. At fourteen I started frying at a chicken restaurant. I decided early on that fryer heat was just too much for me and I moved to more front of the house positions. I worked in the restaurant service industry throughout my teens and twenties. My first real relationship was with a chef. We drank and ate together for years with the appetite of whales. An appetite that could never be fulfilled.

As an adult on my own with one child, our kitchen was small. It was always tidy and crammed to the gills with an impressive variety of books, family heirlooms, and utensils. I didn't have much time to just sit and watch cooking shows, but I would DVR The Naked Chef, Bizarre Foods with Andrew Zimmerman, Rachel Ray, Anthony Bourdain Parts Unknown, and Man Versus Food.

I attempted to watch Giada's Everyday Italian, but it's hard for me to get enthralled in a chef who looks as if she might blow away. No offence, Giada.

© KONINKLIJKE BRILL NV, LEIDEN, 2020 | DOI: 10.1163/9789004441651_035

Maybe I'm just envious of the way you are immune to carbs.

Cooking is one of the many things I have tried to teach my son. I told him that cooking is reading, measuring, and following directions. If you can do that, you can pretty much cook anything.

I introduced him to different things so he could discover himself. Things like baseball, basketball, and swimming. He would participate, but I had to remind him to practice. However, cooking drew him in without coaxing.

My son's childish hands learned quickly how to decorate cookies, measure and add ingredients, stir and even chop. He would read recipes out loud and ask questions while music played softly in the background.

"Mom, what is this word?" he would ask while pointing accurately with his index finger.

"That word is dredge and it means to cover with flour." I would ask his opinion on recipes.

"Kenny, what do you think would go better with the pecan Belgian waffles, blueberries or raspberries?"

"Raspberries, I still remember. They turned out delicious.

Kenny also has bold and adventurous taste buds. He wasn't leary of calamari, sushi, or any other seafood for that matter. My child likes mushrooms. How many kids actually like mushrooms? You would have had to threaten to incinerate all of my Cabbage Patch Dolls to even get me to lick a mushroom as a child.

Cooking and dining out has been a journey with my son. We were the kind of people that took pictures of our food and bragged about it. We agreed that food should be appealing to the taste and sight. We couldn't help but get excited when a cake was artistically frosted or even when a salad is fresh and colorful.

Looking back, I'm glad I took advantage of those moments. Kenny's dad was around, but he was emotionally unavailable. So in many ways, I had to fill two pairs of shoes. I tried to be a nurturing mother, as well as do my best to teach him how to grow up to be a man. I believe that everyone, including every man, should know how to cook.

Years later, my son towers over me. He's a teenager, and the prison system I'm currently in is not supportive of our relationship. I barely get to see or talk to him. When I do talk to him, he tells me about all the dishes he plans to prepare for me, about the new restaurants in the area. One morning, I told him how I was craving lemon bars. There was a pause.

"Um, hello?"

"Oh my gosh, mom, that is so creepy. I literally just finished making lemon bars."

Are our taste buds and bellies connected telepathically? Hmm, who knows. It would be cool if they were. What I do know is that anyone has the ability to sew seed in the most insignificant of moments in their everyday life. We can nourish someone's soul and body just by being genuine and present. Scents and flavors leave impressions that can overpower distance and time.

It's safe to say that I will never have my own cooking show. Or my own restaurant, for that matter. Honestly, I never wanted either of those things. All I wait for now is to get back to the place where my son reads recipes to me with music playing softly in the background.

CHAPTER 35

Unanswered Questions

Paiten Hamilton

October 23, 2017

Dear Diary,

> Do you love me?
> Do you love me not?
> Question lingers in the air
> Until my heart rots

Sitting in my room thinking about this relationship. We've been together for two years. At first everything seemed perfect, but now I'm not so sure. We've had our fights, but I never thought it would come to this. These thoughts that I can't explain keep flourishing in my mind over and over again. But they are not only thoughts. They are feelings. Less confident, less myself, less happy with my life. I know that I love you but, I don't know if I love myself enough. After all the things I've been through with relationships, they all have something in common. The common factor is me feeling like I need that person more than I need myself. This situation is the same, but I have never been put in the position to choose. You or Me. If I leave you to find that love, then you'll be heartbroken. So I'll just stay and hold on a little longer. I can love us both at the same time... Right?

January 3, 2018

Dear Diary,

> True love will find you but,
> I'm IT, in a game of hide and seek

As time goes on, my mind keeps running. I can't help but to think about what I am feeling and why. Love is causing me a lot of pain right now. I was wrong, I can't love us both at the same time because here I am losing sleep thinking about how unhappy I am. But I am also confused on why because you're a good man to me. I don't want to lose our friendship and our bond. You have a great heart and would never hurt me. So why would I hurt you by leaving you?

Why do I feel the need to always make decisions based on the other person's interest? I need to be honest with you, but most importantly honest with myself.

January 24, 2018

Dear Diary,

Searching through a pile of daisies

It feels like my days are getting longer. I can't seem to stay out of my mind. Feeling vacant because the lack of a feeling that only I can give to myself. But why is it so hard? Why can't I seem to give it to myself? Why? These are the things that I think about nowadays. I know that I don't love myself as much as I should and this relationship is making it harder for me.

The thoughts continue to linger when I'm asleep; the underlying message lingers in my dreams. My tooth is loose. But when I wake, it's there. I am so confused. Looking up the meaning, it says that I am afraid to lose something that means so much to me. And it is very accurate. I don't want to lose him, but I don't want to lose myself either.

I have to break up with him to bring peace to myself.

February 10, 2018

Dear Diary,

Power sits in your palm
Yet, I can't get a good grip

I'm scared. I'm scared of the change that'll come with me leaving you. Will you hate me? Will I break your heart? Why is that what's holding me back from making this decision that I can't shy away from. Why?

I have the power to free myself from these chains. But the fear of what will happen after is the key. I have to let go and let God do his work, no matter the fear. Tomorrow.

February 15, 2018

Dear Diary,

After months of dwelling on the issue of should I stay for you or leave for me, it was time. I can't hold on to it anymore. I need myself more than I need you. That doesn't mean that I don't love you, it just means that I want to love me more. I have to face this fear for the sake of myself. I have to let you go to find myself. Self love is important and I can't take it anymore. In the words of Joyce Marter, "Self Love Must Come First."

I finally had the courage to do it. I broke it off over FaceTime, which was probably the worst way to do it. Now all I can do is hope. Hope that we both find peace, love and happiness again.

"Knowing yourself is the beginning of all wisdom"—Aristotle

When reading an article by Adam Smith, he stated that there are 6 steps you need to take in order to know your true self. One of those that stuck out to me the most was to BE QUIET. What he meant by that is to take the time to be still. Stating that being alone is uncomfortable but being alone allows you to evaluate yourself and be truthful with every facet of your life.

Another part of this article that stuck with me is to ASSESS YOUR RELATIONSHIPS. Going into detail on what that means is a large aspect of knowing yourself can be found in the relationships you have with people.

The part that really related to my situation was when he said "When you realize you'll never truly know anyone else until you discover yourself, the importance of knowing yourself becomes even more apparent." That's how I feel about love. I realized that I can't love someone else unless I loved myself first.

April 24, 2018

Dear Diary,

I've been doing well. We're both doing good! We are both happy and we have found our way without one another. We are still friends and that's what matters most to me.

I've been using some of Melanie Greenberg's steps to self-love to keep me sane.
- Recognizing when I am experiencing emotional distress
- Accepting my feelings
- Self-Talk to encourage myself

I also pay very close attention to myself, my thoughts, and my body. I am more accepting of who I am because I can't change it. I have been the happiest I've ever been in a while.

References

Greenberg, M. (2017). 8 powerful steps to self-love. *Psychology Today.* Retrieved from https://www.psychologytoday.com/us/blog/the-mindful-self-express/201706/8-powerful-step s-self-love

Marter, J. (2016). Self-love must come first: How to love yourself. *HuffPost.* Retrieved from https://www.huffingtonpost.com/joyce-marter-/selflove-must-come-first-_b_9237282.html

Smith, A. (2016). 6 steps to discover your true self. *Success.* Retrieved from https://www.success.com/article/6-steps-to-discover-your-true-self

CHAPTER 36

Gregory's Gift

Sandra Brown

I've never climbed any crystal stairs, son,
But poetry kidnapped me;
Penned me with passion
As precious as pearls.
Spectrums most vibrant fade
In comparison to Langston Hughes.
Bright like an eyeful of sun.
Dark like midnight at the corner
Of nowhere and nothing.
It kisses your ears with Jazz music,
Smells like a coffee house,
Feels crazy, rocky, sexy, cozy.

How do I love thee?
Sense and see.
Sample some Elizabeth Barrett Browning
And a slice of Shakespeare.
Stop by Frost's "Woods on a Snowy Evening;"
Thaw from the fire of Giovanni's Pen.

I give you Poe's Raven,
Brooke's Maude Martha,
Dunbar's Mask,
And my conversation with Rosa Parks.

We are yours.
Make history.
Make legacy.
Make poetry.

CHAPTER 37

Sentimental Syrup

Cara Quiett

It was a searing hot summer, especially in our double-wide trailer. I wake up before anyone, like I usually did. I scavenged for something to eat before I bothered to drag a brush through my teeth and sun-bleached hair.

There was not usually much of anything at all. It helped that I knew how to cook. At this particular memory, I was nine at that point in my life. I could cook basic things like macaroni and cheese, eggs, French toast, and pancakes. Pancakes were one of the very first things I learned to cook.

I preferred the toast of French toast to pancakes, but I enjoyed making pancakes more. There is more skill required. I used to play a game with myself when I would pour batter into the hot skillet and randomly move my arms around to create different shapes with the batter. I prided myself on my ability to make THE BEST Mickey Mouse shaped pancakes.

Luckily for me, we had pancake batter, along with the required ingredients. But… did we have syrup? Yep, wonderful! My sunken stomach was doing somersaults and the prospect of food. A much celebrated, yet sparse occurrence at our humble abode.

The rule was, I was not supposed to use the stove without an adult present. However, I was hungry. By that time I had figured out that as long as I was quiet and did not make a mess. Rules would be bent and shaped to accommodate my needs.

I no longer had to read the Jiffy mix box to know the items that I need. I always double-checked the mix to make sure no weevils had infested the floury substance. Once I had made the mistake of wasting batter that was buggy before. Not only could I not eat the pancakes, but I wasted two eggs. That will never happen again.

To prevent my hungover mom and step-dad from waking, I would gingerly extract the items from the cabinets and refrigerator. It felt like I was playing an intense game of Operation. Despite my efforts, I heard a muffled thud. Darn, I woke up my two-year-old brother. I could tell by the staggering pad of his steps and squishy diaper sounds.

My waking endeavor had just gotten a bit more complicated. Instead of keeping myself quiet it was my responsibility to keep him quiet too. My brother, Christopher, looked like Oppie Taylor if Oppie was a r******, stout,

© KONINKLIJKE BRILL NV, LEIDEN, 2020 | DOI: 10.1163/9789004441651_038

sumo wrestler. For a wee man of his stature, he was surprisingly light on his feet. He was almost as sneaky as me.

He saw me. I put my finger to my lips to form the universal sign for shhhh and pointed to his high chair. He climbed his high chair like the puff marshmallow man climbing the Empire State Building in the original Ghostbusters movie. My brother was the bane in my existence and also the most beautiful thing I had ever seen. I would cradle him to sleep sometimes and become hypnotized by the way his long blonde lashes fluttered during his dreams.

I knew he would be thirsty so I poured him a cup of Kool-Aid. He chugged it effortlessly and released a refreshed exasperation. He extended his pudgy hand with the cup to gesture for more of the cheap, sugary, beverage. As his own personal bartender, I obliged and poured him a bit more but told him "That's it. I have to make breakfast." He did not protest as he waited patiently with his berry blast mustache. Like a compact wise adult, he gazed out the window to the rising sun. He wore the blue mustache throughout the day, along with other evidence of his adventures.

Before I could reach the stove, I had to get a milk crate to stand on. The one we had was also the place where we would pile our shoes. It was in front of our dog's kennel. My dog, Ditka, woke up because he had figured out that if I am getting a crate, I must be cooking and he was all too willing to snatch up any spills or drops. If I burned something, which was not often, he would get that too. I had stopped giving him food scraps for a while because he was turning into a food bully. Ditka had gobbled up my peanut butter and jelly when I had gone to answer the phone and when I offered him a lick of my nutty buddy ice cream cone, his greedy butt chomped the entire thing and almost took off my hand. However, he was smart and could sense what a sucker I was for his dark, weary eyes. He woke up, crawled out of his kennel and observed as I transferred the shoes from the crate so I could use the crate as my pedestal to reach the stove.

Our kitchen was a nook of broken cookware and torture devices. Wooden spoons were skull crackers, spatulas were thigh, butt, and face slappers, pepper grinders, creamer pots, gravy boats and anything else not bolted down could have been seen sailing through the air at any time. This is why we could not have nice things. The clock on our microwave did not work because someone decided to smash someone else's head into it. Our tiny kitchen was frequently the scene of a bar brawl. But hey, at least it could still make a bean and cheese burrito.

Once I dug through the rusted and broken utensils and collected what I needed, it was time to mix the batter. The recipe called for a cup of mix here, a couple of eggs, vegetable oil and milk. After I stirred the batter until it was no longer lumpy it was time to spark up the stove.

The only leftover pan we owned was on the stove as I turned the knob. Tick, tick, boom as the blue and orange flames blossomed beneath the bottom of the pan. So far, things were going well. Lighting the stove would be tricky for me back then. I had singed my aquanet bangs before causing an impromptu haircut. I turned the flame down to half mass. I had already discovered that burnt butter ruins the taste of pancakes.

With a butter knife, I sliced a teaspoon tab of butter from the half-melted butter stick and schlepped it onto the heated pan. I rolled the butter around and watched it dissolve into a sheen that covered the pan. It reminded me of the spring days during recess when our blacktop basketball court shimmered from a downpour.

Some people like silver dollar pancakes, but I liked them bigger. One of my favorite treats was the eraser to thumb size bites that drip off the edge of the bowl. Like staring at the clouds and looking for an animated story to unfold in the seemingly endless sky. I asked myself, "What could it be, what could it be?" I held the doughy pieces in my buttery palm and brought them to my brother.

"Look Chris, this one kind of looks like Homer Simpson, and this one looks like Frankenstein." I blew on them before we popped them into our hungry mouths. Appetizers before our entrees.

You know a pancake is ready when the edges bubble and you can slide an ass slapper underneath it easily without it falling apart. They taste the best when they are just a tad lighter than a graham cracker. After a few flips and turn-overs, the stack was ready. I knew the perfect bite size pieces to make for Christopher. I have always saturated my pancakes in syrup and could never understand them being eaten any other way.

Despite my skills, there was one slightly scorched jack that I dropped in the dog's bowl. It was gone before I even made it back to the table. The dog, being, the opportunist food bully he was, approached my brother's high chair for seconds. My baby brother scowled with his gilded eyebrows. I sternly pulled Ditka away by his collar into the living room, which was only a few feet away. He surrendered and curled up on the couch.

We ate peacefully. Christopher's chubby digits brought soggy bites to his cherub face. Syrup rolled down his buddha belly and onto his ample thighs. We were full for a little while.

Lately, for the past six years and nine months. I woke up every Wednesday around four-thirty a.m. for pancakes. It is way earlier than I would ever get up, but since I am nostalgic, I find the smallest resemblance of comfort in this simple food and go out of my way to get it. I pray and slide out of my bunk. I brush my teeth and hair. A small regular group of us march slowly, two by two, down a dinge hallway while playing red-light, green-light. I glance out the windows to catch the sunrise pastels.

Mall cop correctional officers direct us and stare at us like we are zoo creatures. The kitchen supervisors, no matter who he/she is, always look pissed and miserable. We stand in line and wait for our state portion of two pancakes, a scoop of grits, two margarines, an ounce packet of diabetic syrup, two four-ounces powdered milks and a four-ounce juice.

I'll occasionally gently nod and smile at a friendly face, but usually I don't say or do much. It is too damn early, but it is another day closer to home. Once I have collected my tray and spork, I look to the officer to guide me where I sit. I straddle my seat and pray again. I have never been fond of communal seating. The elbow stabbing and open mouth chewing is enough to make you wish you had the gift to projectile vomit like Reagan from The Exorcist. To get through it, I sometimes pretend I'm at a hibachi restaurant. Most of the time, I take deep breaths and focus on myself. At least we are not usually hostages to the chow hall for long.

About seven minutes tops, especially in the morning.

It does not take long to eat my measly pancakes. I could wolf down four as a small child. What can I say, I have a hearty appetite for the things that I like. It has gotten me in trouble throughout my life. At least, through this experience, I have learned to be grateful for every morsel. People awaken starving everyday and I understand their hunger.

My brother has not spoken to me since my incarceration. I heard he got engaged this past New Year. I miss the days when he was the bane of existence. It is funny what you miss. I dangerously ponder why he has shut me out. Maybe he does not know what to say to me. Perhaps he is embarrassed or worse. Maybe I remind him too much of our mother, a woman he has not been able to forgive in over twenty years.

To keep the pain at bay, I reached these thoughts deep into my mind. I absorb the moments like syrup into pancakes.

CHAPTER 38

Perfection: A History of Me & My Multi-Colored Elephants

Kathryn A. Coffey

Onychophagia

This piece started with a poem that I wanted to turn into a song. Even then, the only lines that I could always remember were "I can't get enough of you. I'm not sure why I do." It would have been some sort of metaphor for a crappy relationship, like one of those bitter Taylor Swift love ballads or something like that. But being a Taylor Swift-like song writer seems like a pathetic goal to go for. Maybe Bob Dylan is a better choice. But then again, no one could be Bob Dylan in a day. BUT, I digress. There's an elephant in the room that needs addressing. You can say there are a bunch of multi-colored elephants in the room that I need to address all at once.

• • •

All my life, numbers were always a drag, but there are a lot of things I remember doing both to stop me from hurting myself and letting myself be hurt. Sloppily painted, very short, and slightly dirty, they have been a pain in the neck for as far back as I can remember. I've painted over them many times. Every time I paint them, the paint always chips off, partly because my fingers can't stop picking at them. I always hated my nails, but for the time being, I don't want to do any more damage than I have done already.

This is my fifth or sixth time—or maybe it's the third or fourth time. I don't know. I never bother to keep track of these things. As I said before, numbers are totally bogus. What matters more to me is remembering what actually happened.

The numbers can always come later.

• • •

My brother was giving my mother a hard time. He didn't want his nails clipped. I'm not sure if I thought I could do a better job at maintaining my own nails

© KONINKLIJKE BRILL NV, LEIDEN, 2020 | DOI: 10.1163/9789004441651_039

than my mom's clippers or the distress I experienced seeing my brother struggle. Either way, this was the moment I started a long, arduous journey with the addiction of onychophagia, or, as everyone else calls it, nail-biting.

Although I never really kept track of my age until I was around ten years old, if I were to give a guess, I've been biting them since I was around five or six, which would make it fourteen/fifteen odd years. Which begs the question: why have I been chewing on my nails for so long?

Well, the underlying cause of nail-biting has always been unclear, mainly because it's underrecognized, meaning it's a habit without a definite cause. But if someone were to give an educated guess, it might have to do with feeling stressed out. In their article "Nail Biting: A Habit or a Disease?," Taleb and Shaarani state, "The principal psychological factors found to be associated with this behavior are stress, nervousness, anxiety, and low mood" (medscape.com). In that case, if I deal with anxious thoughts I'm thinking about, maybe I'll be able to beat it. But the thing is, there's something about seeing people biting their nails in stressful situations that get me laughing.

When I see cartoon characters chewing on their nails, I find it funny in a schadenfreude kind of way. It's not me being a bad ruler of France whose subjects don't really like very much (such as in the Animaniacs episode "Three Muska-Warners") or being chastised by another kid my age of the opposite sex for not doing the job as efficiently as he could (such as in the Codename: Kids Next Door episode "Operation F.U.G.I.T.I.V.E."). Because I find it funny, I thought others could find it funny, too. But being in those stressful places in life isn't exactly fun, and it's something that doesn't guarantee a laugh in real life. So naturally, when a joke doesn't work, I should just drop it, right? But here's the thing: it's kind of hard to stop what I've already started fourteen/fifteen years ago. On top of which, there are always more reasons that pile up every day compelling me to keep up a horrible habit.

• • •

Sometimes life leaves me frustrated, and sometimes, I can't fully elaborate on why that is. I don't want to burden anyone with what I'm feeling, so I suppose it's easier for me to vent my frustration of the world around me on my nails. There are times where I want to speak, but half the time, it would be about something that had nothing to do with anything. Asking people to hang out is always a hassle; all my friends have their own lives to live, and I tell myself that they'd probably be too busy doing more important stuff than hanging out with me.

And besides, who would want to hang out with a nail-biter?

Sure, I do get to hang out, but very rarely do I ask people to hang out outside of the organizations I'm a part of. I remember one of my friends saying if I ever need to have time to myself, she would understand, but what she doesn't know, and what I wanted to tell her, is I always have time to myself and I'm sick of it. There's the picture-perfect image of people hanging out together, and it's something that I can never achieve.

Does that mean I'm a perfectionist? It probably would be according to Susan Cosier. Her article "Nail Biting May Arise from Perfection," mentions that people who bite their nails have a habit of wanting the perfect image. In a study of forty-eight people, half with anxiety-related disorders and the other without them, she states, "Those with the disorders scored as organizational perfectionists, indicating a tendency to over plan, overwork themselves and get frustrated quickly without high levels of activity" (Cosier).

Maybe that was my friend's way of saying I was overworking myself, even though I wasn't really feeling like it. Then again, overworking is something I tend to do a lot. Besides, the angsty/jealousy feeling I get usually lasts only for a few moments before I start to feel contentment with where I am, and I finally enjoy the moment.

While I'm happy with where I am most of the time, as with anyone, I get jealous of people who have what I do not. On top of which, the landscape is always changing. My friends are getting married. Couples meet up and break apart just as quickly. I changed my major. My school is not a fifteen-minute drive away from home anymore. At least with nail-chewing, there's a sense that at least some things never change. I would always have my short, ugly, dirty, and all-around unpleasant nails to have and to chew on. Having it not be the case has been a long haul from the beginning.

The first time I considered quitting this habit of biting my nails was when

I went to St. Linus, a Catholic grammar school. Before I went there, I went to Stony Creek Elementary, a public grammar school. At the time I was there, I didn't remember caring too much about the people around me, so I would always bite my nails. I didn't care who was watching. The only reason I switched schools was my parent's insistence that I get actual mathematics instead of the type of mathematical education I was getting, which I guess was none, but not like I ever cared.

St. Linus is where I started to care a little more about my appearance. It was the fifth grade—or maybe middle school—and one of my teachers was holding a spa session for students. The teacher was new and young, just like me at that time. The nail polish looked nice and I wanted to join in on the fun, but here was the problem: my nails were very short. They weren't long like the other girls. Even so, they were washed and painted and they actually started to look nice.

In middle school, there was only one other kid that still bit his nails. He even picked his nose. He wore glasses, had short, platinum blonde hair, and everyone knew him as Matt: a very crusty kid. He was also an oddball. As a teenager, I didn't mind being an oddball, but I didn't want that to be known as crusty.

A while later, after they were painted, I saw my nails grow a bit. They at least looked longer than Matt's nails. But they still looked ugly and not that clean. I didn't bother to get a nail-cleaning kit for myself, but one thing led to another, and the next thing I know, I'm back to square one.

• • •

Since that day, I've been painting my nails in order to stop me from biting them. It always succeeds... for a couple of weeks. As for why I didn't try anything else, well, I'm a college student. I don't have time to deal with this crap as it is. And with no other options I knew, I start to pick at them again. I don't want to bite them, because of the colorful polish. But once the polish is all gone or very much eroded away, the picking turns into biting. After a while, the cycle starts all over again.

Recovery is going to take some time, but at least I'm not the only one who struggles to break the habit. In her article, "Nail Biting: Mental Disorder or Just a Bad Habit?" Amy Standen explains how she may have stopped herself from biting her nails, but it's still a struggle to keep her then three-year old daughter from falling into the trap. She would try to bat her daughter's hands away from her mouth. It got to the point where Standen "[...] had to decide what was worse: making Cora feel bad about herself for something she couldn't help, or just letting her grow into a nail biter, which, while certainly not the worst thing in the world, had given [Standen] some grief" (Standen).

Talk about being stuck between a rock and a hard place. It could be tough to quit something involuntary; however, it begs the question: do you have to bring shame to your identity to be someone you're not?

In the same article, she mentions a colleague who also has a daughter with a nail-biting habit. Her name is Tracy Foose. She's a psychiatrist working in San Francisco and seems to embrace her identity as a nail-biter. She states that because her friend's mother was an artist who bit her nails, she associated nail-biting with not only being cool, but also being a part of growing up (Standen/Foose). It may be interesting to think about, but I beg to differ. There's more to growing up than acquiring a nasty habit. Remember how cool George Harrison looked smoking a cigarette? Well, the fact of the matter is he's dead now, and it's specifically because all that smoking caught up to him in the end. Not saying nail-biting is that hazardous a habit, but at the same time, looking at short nails starts to get embarrassing after a while.

• • •

Recently, I decided to try to be better about quitting, because of my mother. It's not like she asked me to stop directly (though she always asks me to if she catches me doing it), but she has been saying how much she wants to keep to her New Year's resolution more than ever.

In all my years I've known her, she was always off-and-on with her goals, but there was something about these last two years of being away at college that made everything seem different. Freshman year, we had an agreement to have one call every week, and to be honest, after a while I started to run out of things to talk about. There are certain things that happen in college that I would NEVER talk about with my parents. Partly because I'm sure they've seen it before, but mostly because I don't want to blab out my floor's drama to my folks. I'm pretty sure people just don't do that.

And what's more, Mom would always say that she and dad miss me almost every time I visit or call. And of course, I say I would miss them, too. But I guess I never really thought about how me leaving would make them feel, because, for me, the repetition of something nice starts to lose meaning after years of saying it. That's why I don't say that out loud. I guess for them, the meaning never changes, and there's no point if nothing changes. But what the heck do I know? I'm not in their heads. However, there are writers that could give me an idea of what they might be thinking.

In her article "Coping When Your Oldest Kid Goes Off to College," Michelle Newman analyzes standard advice that is often given to help parents cope with what's happening and how emotions can debunk how that advice can make parents feel. She states,

> Is it because you've spent what seems simultaneously like a lifetime making sure your child is ready for this extraordinary milestone and your joy will eventually trump all the anxiety and uncertainty? Sure, but you'll be so completely exhausted emotionally from the year leading up to this moment that you'll be surprisingly relieved to get to the other side. (Newman, 2018)

Back then, Mom must've been missing having the whole family together some-thing fierce while I was out enjoying my freedom. And it must've been some-what emotionally exacerbated when Michael, my younger brother, started college at DePaul.

And when Mom gets emotionally distressed, she would want to keep herself busy. I should know. Not only would I do the same thing, but she would also tell me so on multiple occasions. With Michael and me not being in the house so often anymore, she needed all the distraction she could get. She got herself a planner with colorful pens, as well as a few books on self-improvement. She's even said that if she writes down what she needs to do on a to-do list, they would usually get done in a timely manner. Her coping mechanism translated to me that we can all change. And from there, I decided enough was enough. It was time to kick the nail-biting habit for good.

• • •

Before the spring semester started, I painted my nails. But over time, as always, the paint began to chip. Leaving me those disgusting, short nails I've known for all these years. And yet, now I decide to paint over my nails again, as soon as I got access to nail-polish remover. It doesn't matter that every nail I paint looks like an inkblot orgasm. It doesn't matter the paint would chip away. I don't want to live with this nail-biting issue forever. Seeing my mother's atti-tude toward her goals made me realize that perhaps this attempt to kick this God-forsaken habit off will be different, even if I have this picking problem to reckon with.

When it comes to kicking habits, there's always more than one way to get things done. And if you don't believe me—who used to use only one method of quitting the habit, so why would you believe me anyway—just ask Emily R, who wrote "I Tried 5 Hacks to Stop Biting My Nails, and Only 1 Made a Differ-ence." In her article, she looked up methods on quitting on Reddit, and the var-ious methods she tried included rubbing jalapeños on her fingernails. It didn't get her to completely stop, but what did get the result she wanted was thinking about the bacteria growing in her nails and how much she didn't want to get sick. At the end of her article, she states,

> in day-to-day circumstances, I bite my nails without even realizing I'm doing it a lot of times. That's where the other hacks like salt and jalapeño come in. They may not have turned me away from doing it, but they did make me aware that my hands were in my mouth—which made them beneficial in their own sort of way. (Rekstis, 2018)

Thus, maybe I shocmore awareness of me biting my nails. If I'm more aware of what I'm doing, maybe it'll get me to stop.

Would thinking about the bacteria on my nails work for me? Would thinking about the little germs that rest in my fingernails turn me off to biting them, let alone picking them? Well, I don't think so, especially because I don't get sick too often.

Honestly, if I had it my way, I would get some nail polish that creates optical illusions. So when I bring my nails close to my face, all I could ever see is what I fear most. For the record, it would be either a wasp flying toward me or Nosferatu coming towards the camera. Just your average muggle making some basic Harry Potter shit. And it would be called Fear Factor Nail Polish. But since Harry Potter isn't real, no matter how much Universal Studios might try to convince me otherwise, I suppose I'll have to wait until someone invents something like that.

But something I might do would be the rubber band technique. It's where you wear a rubber band around your wrist like a bracelet. Only, you pull it back and let it slap your wrist when you feel the urge to pick. Going back to using shame to quit the habit, perhaps it's not exactly the best option to go with. In her article "Every Strategy I've Tried to Stop Picking My Cuticles, Ranked," beauty writer Beth Shapouri (2017) gave this method 2.1 out of 10. In her reasoning, she states, "I never would do it because life is short and the only thing I'm harming is the look of my cuticles. And, as The Princess Bride tells us, life is pain, no need to add anything on top of it."

And if quoting movies have taught me anything, it's that they could bring truth, especially when the moment is right. So, where do I go from here?

What I'm doing now is carrying around a nail filer. I remember my Nana would always carry around one of those in her purse and the one I have on me gives off a sense of nostalgia. It's beige cardboard on one side and sparkly orange goodness on the other: just like the one Nana used to have. For some reason, I always had one in my colored pencil box but never bothered to use it. That is, until now, where this time is just as good as any. And besides, I kind of like the way it feels, especially on my left thumb nail.

When I file them, they turn out really short, and it's already making a difference. I'm not feeling the urge to pick so much. The best part is, I could fix my nails without spending a lot of money. Maybe I could get a proper manicure done with my mom, but I'm getting ahead of myself.

If worst comes to worst, I should consult a doctor. It's what you're supposed to do when you can't fix unhealthy things by yourself. It's going to be quite a trip, but it's one I'm going to be willing to take with honor, dignity, and willingness.

References

Cosier, S. (2015, July 01). Nail biting may arise from perfectionism. *Scientific American*. Retrieved from www.scientificamerican.com/article/nail-biting-may-arise-from-perfectionism/

Newman, M. (2018, May 11). *Coping when your oldest kid goes off to college*. Retrieved from https://grownandflown.com/parent-sendingfirstborn-off-to-college/

Rekstis, E. (2018, February 14). I tried 5 Hacks to stop biting my nails and only 1 made a difference. *Self*. Retrieved from https://www.self.com/story/nail-biting-hacks

Shapouri, B. (2017, May 26). Every strategy I've tried to stop picking my cuticles, ranked. *Glamour*. Retrieved from https://www.glamour.com/story/how-to-stop-picking-your-cuticles-tips

Standen, A. (2012, October 01). Nail biting: Mental disorder or just a bad habit? *NPR*. Retrieved from http://www.npr.org/sections/health-shots/2012/10/01/161766321/nail-biting-mental -disorder-or-just-a-bad-habit

Taleb, R. M., & Shaarani, I. A. (2016, May 19). Nail biting: A habit or a disease. *Medscape*. Retrieved from https://www.medscape.com/viewarticle/863395

CHAPTER 39

Final Thoughts

Sandra Brown

I am the sum total of the World.
She disguised me in labels, lies, and stereotypes.

I am the One about which
they all have something to say.
As if they really know me.

I am the purest blue
beating at the heart
of burning candles
moving in the stillness.

In the beginning
I reinvented my Self.
And the mind was without form
and void.
So I said, "Let there be thought,"
and there was thought.

The Angel in the House
tried to seduce me with silence:
Like the Big, Bad Woolf,
I killed her, too.
Blank canvas
gave birth to words,
birth to lines,
birth to verse.
Voice in hand
put form to thoughts,
round,
living like a full womb.

© KONINKLIJKE BRILL NV, LEIDEN, 2020 | DOI: 10.1163/9789004441651_040

I am the difference
no one wanted me to make.
Woman, Black Phoenix,
infinite holder of the stars.
I reinvented my Self.

I am the One about which
they all still have something to say.
My heart still beats
in the stillness of the Night.
My mind labors and gives birth
loudly, daily, freely.

And it is good and very good.

CHAPTER 40

Stopping the Cycle: My Journey with Generational Body Image

Kelly Cunningham

The blaring sound of my iPhone alarm goes off. I let it ring for minutes on end before I can no longer stand the sound. With the blinds closed, my room remains pitch black. I roll over and shut off the monotonous ringing. As I continue to lay in the quiet darkness, I imagine what a delight it would be to rest my eyes and drift back off to sleep. Just as my eyes begin to close, my phone repeats its alarming noise. Tempted to hit the snooze button again, I turn off the alarm and force myself to sit up and rub the sleep out of my tired eyes. I throw my legs over the side of my unmade bed and stumble over to the light switch, which felt like miles away from where I was standing. As I flick on the light, my eyes take time to adjust to the new brightness in the room.

I wonder how my room had gotten so messy after just two days. The piles of clothes that quickly turned into mountains remind me of my least favorite morning task, deciding what I will wear. I try to remember what my clean floor looked like, how it made me feel relaxed and at peace. The clothes scattered across my carpet represent each insecurity that I possess. Each knit sweater, long sleeved dress, and pair of jeans taunt me with cruel words that should only be used to describe the evilest. I make my way over to my closet, dreading the decision I will soon have to make. I flip through each article of clothing three times, never satisfied with what I find. I pull out a deep green sweater and try it on with a pair of jeans. I pull off the top of one of the highest mountain peaks in my bedroom.

I tentatively walk over to the mirror and examine myself from every angle. Immediately hating what I see I pull the sweater over my head and toss it where my pair of jeans once rested. Over and over I continue to try on different options, and I soon begin to taste the salty tears that are rolling down my cheeks. I make my way back to my bed and allow myself a moment to rest and recover. My mind races as I think about ways to change who I am or how I look. As my wheels continue to spin, I look at my phone and notice the time. A jolt of energy hits me as I realize I need to hurry and make it to class on time. I pull myself together and settle on the knit green sweater that I tried on first.

• • •

© KONINKLIJKE BRILL NV, LEIDEN, 2020 | DOI: 10.1163/9789004441651_041

At eight years old, I sat at my Grandma's kitchen table. She was cooking spaghetti as I sat and colored pictures with her box of knock-off crayolas. As the smell of garlic and tomato sauce filled the air, I completed my coloring of four yellow sunflowers in a field. I looked up to see my Grandma serving me a plate of spaghetti, with a side of crispy garlic bread. We chatted about our day as I laughed at myself slurping noodles into my mouth. As the amount of pasta on my plate lessened, she asked if I wanted anymore. I gave my usual response of "no, I'm done" and she gave it about two minutes before asking me again. As she continued to press on, I gave in and allowed her to fix me up a little bit more. As my silly slurping continued my Grandma sat back down and watched me eat.

Displeased with what she saw, she told me, "Kell-bell, if you want to try, I will give you one dollar for every pound you lose."

I immediately stopped eating. Puzzled with why she wanted me to lose weight, I pushed my plate of spaghetti away and said, "okay."

• • •

My sophomore year of high school, I was serenaded in front of my entire class and asked to prom. My excitement bubbled as I thought about buying a flowing gown that I would get to wear. I went home from school that day and asked my mom when we could go prom dress shopping together. The next afternoon my mom, my grandma, and I went out to find that perfect dress. As I walked in there was a sea of tulle and rainbow silk all around me. The rhinestones and sequins shone so bright that I couldn't contain my little girl fantasies of all things sparkly.

As I flipped through the rack, I felt myself looking around to see if anyone was watching what size I took off of the shelf. My arms began to fill up with bright colored dresses, so I asked to use a fitting room and begin the process of trying things on. I was nervous about this shopping process, because I had to walk out of the dressing room and into the open where everyone else who was shopping could see what I looked like in each dress. Potential judgements filled my mind, and I took deep breaths before each entrance into the room. I finally put on a bright coral dress with a sparkly bodice. It was an A-Line cut so it covered up the tummy that I was so insecure about. I felt good. I smiled at myself in the mirror before walking out to show my family. As I walked out, I could see my mom smiling at me and I knew I was so happy with what I had tried on. My Grandma said to me, "I love it, it's so flattering for your shape."

I bought the dress and thought about my shape the whole car ride home.

• • •

A little over two months ago I got a pretty bad case of the stomach flu. I was bedridden for four days and couldn't keep any food down. I had a fever that felt like it would never go away and could not bring myself to sleep through the night. I was desperate for my mom to come take care of me. I couldn't get myself up without feeling faint. I was living off of a lemon-lime soda diet until I realized I was not only sick, but extremely dehydrated. This sickness left me feeling sad and exhausted.

Once this long-lasting bug decided to make its way out of my body, I met up with my family to go on a girl's day. We met about an hour out of where I was and spent the day shopping around. I felt great as I tried on new clothes. It was one of those shopping trips where everything I tried on just happened to look really good. As I got a moment alone with my Grandma, she asked me if I was feeling any better. I let her know that I was so happy to finally be feeling back to normal. I was able to enjoy my day with everyone and feel refreshed. She let me know she was sorry I wasn't feeling well, but on the plus side "it looked like being sick helped you lose some weight!"

In her mind this was a compliment to my figure, in my mind it was just another reminder that I wasn't skinny enough in the first place.

• • •

Body image problems are easily passed down from generation to generation. From mother to daughter, sister to sister, grandmother to granddaughter, the problems are so easily transferred from one person to another. Nearly 40 percent of parents encourage their children to diet (Alexis Conason, Psy. D). This 40 percent is creeping into the minds of their children letting them know that the way they look isn't desirable. It isn't a simple encouragement to be healthy, but instead taking dieting steps in order to change appearance.

Health and appearance are not the same. They do not always correlate. My eight-year-old self felt ugly instead of feeling joyous and free-spirited. I worried about how I looked rather than how I felt. When these ideas are planted into the minds of children at such a young age, the downward spiral begins. At least 30 million people of all ages and genders suffer from an eating disorder in the U.S (Hudson, J. I.). Although different reasons may spark these illnesses, the pressure from family often lends a helping hand to causing these dark thoughts and feelings. Children will look up to their parents. Research has shown that the most important role model in a child's life is the parent of the same sex.

As I think back to my younger years, I recall the way I looked up to my grandma, how she was such a role model for me. Little did I know that her talk about weight, her need to always lose another five pounds, and her quick judgments made on other people about their appearance, would have such an effect on me.

There is a cycle to be broken. History repeats itself, it manifests into the next generation and continuously increases over time. If I could turn back time, I would choose to tell my grandmother the way her words were harming me. It is important for parents to ditch the talk about dieting and focus on making sure their children are living a lifestyle based on feeling good and healthy, rather than maintaining a certain weight and ideal look. It is important to keep talk of weight out of the house, and instead remind kids that beauty comes in all shapes and sizes. Beauty isn't one certain dress size. It isn't about a flat tummy in a bikini. Beauty is about the inside and the warm colors in one's heart. "Model body compassion. Children take in what we put out in the environment. If we focus on treating our bodies (and ourselves) with compassion and respect, our kids will likely follow our cue" (Alexis Conason).

As I remember the time I spent with my Grandma, I remember her constant need to talk about how she just needed to lose five more pounds. She was never satisfied with her look. I always wondered why she was so worried about those five pounds. That's less than the weight of the bowling ball I used when we would go to the bowling alley together. Her obsession with these five small pounds made me wonder how much I needed to be losing. Did I need to look smaller?

Should I have been focusing on five more pounds myself?

• • •

June 17, 2018 soon became my new favorite day. The day my niece was born was a day I will never forget. When I held her tiny body in my arms for the first time, tears of joy rolled down my cheeks and onto her innocent face. As I looked at her, I knew that no matter what, she would always be perfect in my eyes. I would never see her as skinny, or chubby, or bulky, or thin. I would just see her as Sawyer. I hope that as a role model in her life, I can show her that she will always be just fine, just the way she is. If she ever asks me how she looks, I will of course tell her that she is nothing short of an absolute vision, but I will be steady in reminding her that her true beauty comes from the person she chooses to be and the kindness that is in her heart. For my heart will forever worry about hers.

The importance of positive body talk became so real to me the moment I saw her for the first time. I never want her to feel badly about herself because I will always see her as the most perfect person in my life.

References

Benbow, D. H. (2013). Experts: Mom has biggest impact on girls' body image. *USA Today*. Retrieved from https://www.usatoday.com/story/news/nation/2013/08/23/moms-daughters-influence-body-image/2 90921/

Conason, A. (2018). How diet talk can harm your future grandchildren. *Psychology Today*. Retrieved from www.psychologytoday.com/us/blog/eating-mindfully/201804/how-diet-talk-can- harm-Your-future-grandchildren

Hudson, J. I., Hiripi, E., Pope, H. G., & Kessler, R. C. (2007). The prevalence and correlates of eating disorders in the national comorbidity survey replication. *Biological Psychiatry, 61*(3), 348–358.

Porterfield, A. (2017, June 2). I was blindsided by my son's body image issues (it's not just a girl thing). *Scary Mommy*. Retrieved from www.scarymommy.com/boys-have-body-image-issues-too/

Spencer, S. (2017, August 8). How I'm breaking free of my family's vicious cycle of diet culture. *The Mighty*. Retrieved from https://www.themighty.com/2017/08/family-diet-culture-eating-disorder/

CHAPTER 41

My Four Opportunities to Grow Up

Noah Villarreal

Life sends you crazy signals when it's time to grow up. Whether these coming-of-age moments came naturally or were forced upon me, these events lead me to the product I am today. Which, if you were to ask me on any random day, I honestly wouldn't consider myself a "responsible adult." I don't know how to file taxes or apply for a mortgage. I rarely remember to schedule my own doctor's appointments without my mother chiming in to remind me. But then again, are all of these trivial things the signs of being an adult? Are these tasks the markers on your progression to adulthood? Is there really this well-rounded formula to fit the stereotype of being an adult? Of course not. Every person has their own journey to adulthood. However, the following things undoubtedly turn you into what I believe is an adult. And the first step has to be the moment you start truly thinking for yourself.

Original Thought

It's the moment you first said, "Now wait a minute," to a piece of information that you received. Throughout all our childhood, we are given information from elders to help us grow smarter. Others had this information boiled down to the simple, "Share your toys with someone else!" Personally, my moment of Original Thought came in Bible school.

Coming from a Half-Mexican/Half-Irish family from Texas, you can imagine that I received a deep and thorough education of our religious scripture. This included some outside of the classroom readings that was instilled upon me by my father. I will never forget the day I read a passage that I just didn't understand. It's in the book of Timothy. The passage reads exactly, "I do not permit a woman to teach or to have authority over a man; she must be silent." 11 year-old Noah officially wasn't a sheep to the automatic word of his elders. I was raised by a strong woman in my mother. A woman who co-ran her own business with my father. For me to believe for one second that this woman shouldn't have any authority is absolutely absurd.

© KONINKLIJKE BRILL NV, LEIDEN, 2020 | DOI: 10.1163/9789004441651_042

On the way to Bible school, I struck the conversation up with my father. I mentioned the passage to him and he replied, "Some parts we don't listen to. It's a really old book that was written in a different world."

"If it's a really old book then how come we haven't updated it? How come people still listen to the advice given from the same man?" I questioned.

I can't remember exactly what my father replied that, but I do remember it wasn't the most spirited attempt. He could see it from a mile away. I was starting to question things and think for myself, and he knew that my time in the church was going to be a short-lived one. You see, when you start thinking for yourself, you start acting for yourself.

Obtaining Responsibility

When you start acting for yourself, you learn rather quickly that there are consequences from every action you commit. Every moment could be the root cause of another so you must act wisely. And while I didn't learn the consequences of my actions immediately, over time as I look back, I understand what happened in the wringer that is middle school.

First day of middle school; a whole heap of new kids, some you recognize from little league sports, some look like they can already drive. All together this can be a lot to handle for an impressionable kid like I was. And I realized just how impressionable I was when I walked into my first biology class with my new classmate, Justin Cox. Justin Cox said the first cuss words I had ever heard from someone my age within the first minute of meeting him. He greeted me and went on to say, "Aw shit! That faggot Tristan is in this class. Have to stare at his faggot ass all day." And like wildfire, the hate and slander spread amongst these 11 year old boys who really had it out for Tristan McConnell. Using my deduction skills, I gathered the information that Justin and Tristan used to go to the same school and that Tristan is generally hated and Justin is generally liked (despite his awful mouth). This was the moment I made an action without thinking about the consequences. I joined in. Called him a gay-wad or whatever middle school insult when Justin looked at me to chime in. It was that moment I felt like a true follower instead of a leader.

The years went on. I never really even talked to Justin Cox anymore. No one really did come high school because to be frank, everyone thought he was a huge dick. Myself included. What's funny though is that my relationship with Tristan budded in the coming years. He was involved in the theatre department that I was in. I never looked back at that interaction on the first day of school in 6th grade until one night in my sophomore year of high school. Tristan and I were backstage during a tech run of our school musical, so we had a lot of downtime to just talk. I somehow brought up the conversation of, "How'd you come to terms with your sexuality?" And the details he told me about that saga in his life really dug into me. The kid spent all of middle school as an outcast because he didn't feel like he could express who he really was. Boys didn't want to hang out with him because they didn't want to be labeled as his boyfriend, and a lot of girls didn't bother to give him the time of day due to trying to make an impression on the boys. He went on to tell me that he was kicked out of his parents' house for 2 weeks when he finally told them. I can't imagine feeling vulnerable enough to open up your biggest secret to the people that are supposed to love you the most unconditionally in the world, and they reject you. All my mind could trace back is that if he had more people in his corner. If he had more support than the kid who drags down others, maybe the rejection from his parents would have been easier. I don't know how these things work. But I do know that I didn't help his problem. Is it directly my fault for his struggles with coming to terms with his sexuality? No. But it's hard for me to forget that choice I made. That choice I made that had little to no impact on my social standing and had a heavy impact on his. I acted in a situation out of selfishness for my own reputation. And by default, it helped make his worse. I took action at that time. And I felt responsibility for it later.

Awareness of Others

In high-school, I was faced with the predicament of party culture. Something that 16-year-olds don't understand at that age is that drinking is fun, but also can be the root of horrible decisions. One of those decisions took place on the night of my senior prom.

I was dating a Junior named Jessica Lewis at the time. She was a really nice and genuine girl always looking for laughs and a good time. We started dating in January that year and prom fell on a weekend in late April. This particular friend group that we were attending with, truly went all out on the night. Some of their parents booked reservations at this steak house, pictures at this country club lake, and an after party hosted by a friend whose parents were "conveniently" out of town; all of this being escorted by a bougie stretch party limo-bus. Glitz and glamor truly reigned upon our pubescent bodies that evening.

We were sitting at this reserved VIP table at this steak house and the waiter comes and offers us wine. The rest of the group is hesitant to order because well, we're all underage. Except for Dalton Shoemaker who speaks out, "Double Decker Malbec for the whole table." And without hesitation the waiter goes off to fulfill his task. Now personally, I was no stranger to drinking at this time. My girlfriend however, her first drink was a month prior to that evening. To be frank, I didn't think that she was going to drink at all that night. But before I knew it, this girl had downed 3 glasses before we left the restaurant. Those were the first drinks of one of the heaviest displays of drinking I had ever seen.

Flashforward to the after-party. After this huge beer-pong tournament, everyone is with their respective dates, some in bedrooms, some outside. Jessica asks me if I want to go up to find a room and I replied with a quicker yes than ever before. My mind was racing about this experience because up to this point, we hadn't had sex. Pretty much we'd experienced most other things except for the "home run." Maybe this would be the night it all clicks?

We essentially stumble our way upstairs into a room and we start kissing, something is off. Something's off with her mouth aim, something's off with pretty much the whole vibe. She starts unbuckling my pants and I just had to stop her. It wasn't feeling like a genuine interaction between us and I wanted to know what was wrong. The instant that I told her to stop she immediately burst out in tears. I asked her what was wrong and she replied, "I'm sorry I wanted give you a good prom night it's just…" And at that moment I felt so sad for her. She felt pressured and prompted to give me something that she wasn't ready to give. The social pressures of the age-old tale of "getting laid on prom night" really got through to her as if it was something that she had to do. For some reason, I couldn't help but feel like it was my fault somehow. No, I never directly even asked her to do anything, but that look on her face of un-comfortability was something I'll never forget. For the rest of the night, we laid down in our full prom attire looking up at the ceiling talking. She explained to me essentially what it is to be a girl in high school. What it is to be a junior girl dating a senior boy in 2015.

After that night, I looked around at all of my friends differently. With graduation upon us and everything that we had learned up to this point in our lives, there was still so much we didn't know. And we wanted to hide the fact that we didn't know so bad, at all costs. I felt as if I could see everyone as transparent as possible. I learned that everyone's going through their own shit at all times. Whether it be an argument with a loved one, a divorce in the house, or the societal pressures of what a girl should do with her virginity. Thanks to Jess, I feel like I can see everyone a little more clearly now.

Self-Acceptance

As I referenced earlier, I'm involved with theatre. Actually, I'm not just involved, I'm kind of in love with theatre. But I didn't really accept that in myself until much later in life. There're somethings that are really cool to be open about in Austin, Texas, and theatre isn't one of them.

The way that I would mask my theatre-isms was through my friends. I would never hang out with anyone in the theatre department outside of class. EVER. I didn't want to be seen with them and associated with them. I didn't want to separate from the current clique that I was devoted to. The Lacrosse/Football/Basketball friend group that I had had since around 6th grade. Otherwise known as the jocks. Cliques make such a weird vibe in a high school yet they are almost synonymous with each other. I liked where I stood socially and I thought that being associated with some theatre geeks would only drag my rep down. In Jerry Adler's research on high school cliques, it states that "About 20% of students in any school are highly liked, and about 50% are average, meaning that they have some friends, but not necessarily many. The rest are considered neglected or rejected." I felt like I was in the 20% and I didn't want that to change. Up until I got nominated for something that I did in theatre, that's what changed me.

I was nominated for Best Supporting Actor in a Musical in my Junior year and honestly, I didn't know what to make of it. Other than the fact I had to go to a whole heap of rehearsals for this award show that I was dreading immensely. Why am I forced to go to more theatre stuff when I've already done a good job with said theatre gig?? I didn't get it. I was frustrated and in an awful mood at that first rehearsal. I was around a bunch of theatre kids that I didn't know at all. But then they started actually rehearsing.

Some theatre kids from around the area were selected to serve as the ensemble for the show, so they had been rehearsing for this thing for months on in and out. Junior year Noah would've hated all of those rehearsal times and theatre interactions. But a year later, Senior Noah found himself in the selected ensemble for the same awards show. What changed? I saw them perform. The look on their faces, the interaction between actors, everything. They looked like they were truly living their best lives with their best friends doing what they do best. And I wanted that. I wanted to be proud of what I did too.

Then on, I stopped going to so many parties. I auditioned for outside of school work. I was so intently focused on what I could do onstage. I accepted the fact that I am a thespian and I'm freaking proud of it. My jock friends asked me why I didn't spend so much time with them, why I wasn't caring about them. And it wasn't that I didn't care about them. I ended up going to prom with them and having countless other interactions. I just made a change in priority. I started prioritizing myself and my growth as a person and not what others thought I should be. Come senior year, I'm watching musicals every weekend, getting a repertory book ready for college auditions, I was focused. I felt like an artist. I felt like the Noah I should have been for 18 years.

Throughout my life, I find that it's important to reflect, dissect, and accept. Look back on past interactions that might not have meant anything at the time and find meaning in them. Whether it be finding your own belief, realizing your words mean something, a drunken prom night confusion, or accepting who you are. Without the ability to look back, we won't have the opportunity to learn. The opportunity to grow up.

References

Adler, J. (1999). The truth about high school. *Newsweek, 133*(19), 56.

N. A. (2002). *Holy Bible: Containing the old and new testaments.* Oxford University Press.

CHAPTER 42

My Last Bow

Amanda Minetti

When I look over my stand, I see a large crowd through the stage lights and remember feeling nothing.

Click. The case opened, and my eyes beamed at an instrument that was so beautiful it was almost glowing. The instructor, in one swift movement, picks it up, rubs the rosin on the bow and strikes the strings with a beautiful sound that, to this day, rings in my ears.

"Mom! Can I please play the cello!?"

"How about the viola or the violin," she says, looking at the cost of the cello rental compared to the smaller instrument.

I did not know that day would define one of the largest parts of my life.

What are string instruments? String instruments are any musical instrument played by plucking, striking, or drawing a bow across the strings (Merriam-Webster, 2018). There are very few schools that have access to instruments and most music teachers do not even have a room. Instead, they have all of their teaching tools on a cart that they roll around from room to room. When public school funding is cut, the music and art programs are either cut back or completely removed.

According to an article by Joseph Pergola, there has been a steady decline in music programs in public schools since 1997. The problem stems from the economy; if there is no money coming from the taxpayers, then there is no money going into the schools. As public schools are becoming more expensive to operate, it can become a financial burden on the community. The community is the largest source of funding toward public schools through taxes (Pergola, 2014). However, the public is not to blame completely for not funding public schools enough to keep their art programs. Instead, what the government does with the taxpayer money is what makes a difference in school systems. Pergola reflects that, "We must remind everyone the cost of education is far less than the cost of ignorance" (Pergola, 2014).

There are educational benefits to music in public schools that go unrecognized by the people who make the budget cuts. Therefore, their ignorance affects students more than they know by taking away what could be. Music is a safe haven, a stress reliever, and a brain stimulator. The question is; if no one sees any bad values or results coming from a fine arts program, why would we make that part of the budget cut.

When I was young, 9 years old, my school found enough funding to start a music program. In fact, my class was the first ever orchestra of fourth graders at the school. It was a very exciting time for this school of about 500 students. I decided some time later that I, Amanda Minetti, was going to play the violin. My parents, going through their own struggles, found a way to pay for a rented violin. My dad drove me to school at 6:00 AM every morning in the opposite direction of his destination for initial private lessons and my mom would later take me to lessons once a week. To top it all off, they would sit through the pain of listening to 20 fourth graders play Hot Cross Buns and Mary Had A Little Lamb the night of our first concert. My parents saw something I did not. They recognized the value of music.

"Why did you let me play the violin when you could have said no?"

"Because we wanted you to be a well-rounded, cultured person." For that I can never thank them enough.

The benefits of playing an instrument are tremendous, especially for younger children. Learning to play music enhances your memory, math and reading skills, and hand-eye coordination. Playing in a band or orchestra usually involves playing with other students for a certain amount of time a week. During that time students learn how to work as a team and to refine time management and organizational skills. Additionally, students can foster self-expression and view playing as a form to relieve stress (Matthews, 2011). From the standpoint of someone who has played for 11 years, I know these benefits to be true for my first eight years of playing in an orchestra. When things began to get more serious as an upperclassman in high school, we began looking at scholarships and college orchestra. Once the motivation for playing changed, the fun and stress relief of creating music was stripped. Music became stressful and the hours of practicing tiring. The stage fright is not being afraid of a crowd of 100 people but the two professionals sitting across the room listening and watching your every move. Playing in an orchestra is all fun and games until it becomes a matter of business. When I started playing, I did not know that that was what the future held. I just wanted to create music.

By the end of the fourth grade, there were about ten of us left in the orchestra and five of those ten had switched instruments. In fifth grade, kids are eligible to try a band instrument, so we had lost most of our folks to the woodwinds and brass prestige that was somehow the 'cool' thing to do. I remember the people that stayed, because I was one of them, and I remember those folks with whom I played side-by-side for the next nine years. Through thick and thin, we all shared the bond of music, and we became a family in some respects. In high school, we got to travel the states creating memories and experiences that will last a lifetime. By senior year of high school, you could catch me and the other four best players in the class in a practice room at any given moment. We had gotten permission to "work" for our orchestra director during our study hall hour, which was spent practicing, and then we would skip lunch just to spend that time continuously working on our college audition pieces. I am pretty sure I was the only one out of the potential college players that did not want to play in a college orchestra.

However, I soon found myself with a music scholarship at Millikin University and spent every Monday and Wednesday night in the rehearsal room. My orchestral life soon changed as I found that in the midst of professionals, I was easily a very small fish in a big pond.

Music professionals live a slightly different life than those that play for the university, but the level of intensity is about the same. For most professional orchestras, there are a lot of perks that outway the cons. Like all the older colleagues that I played alongside with, there is pay involved. According to PayScale, the average musician makes $39,899 a year, which is less than what the average teacher makes (about $55,000). However, most of these professionals are not in it for the money. There is something about making music that is more satisfying than money. An oboe player named Karen O'Connor who works with a professional orchestra says,

> I think it's because when you start playing a musical instrument, it's a hobby, something you do for real pleasure. Then you get a job, and somebody pays you for it and you think, 'what are my hobbies? What is it I do to make me a balanced person? (Snowdon, 2008)

These professionals are always working. When not at rehearsals, they are practicing or on tour traveling. Having a family can be difficult for these professionals; however, just like any good parent, they still find time for their children. I felt what Karen O'Connor felt—something changed when I entered college as a musician and worked among professionals. I stopped and asked myself, "is this even a hobby anymore?" As for rehearsals, they are nothing like high school rehearsals that I have experienced. In high school, we would get to the rehearsal, chat a little about what we were doing that day, then either sight read or go through rough patches before running the whole piece.

In college, in a professional setting, we are expected to have already practiced our parts and to be familiar with the music before arriving on the first day of rehearsal. There is no chitter chatter, creating a very serious environment. When there was a pause in the music, or the director stopped us to speak, there was a dead silence, not a single bow out of place that would accidentally strike the strings or the cluck of instruments against chairs and stands. We were "professionals."

This was a new world that I had agreed to, and I wasn't sure if I liked it. Professional musicians love what they do because they do not do it for the money, fame, or benefits (which are always nice).

Tears formed in my eyes: "I am sorry, but I just can't do this anymore."

"You are a stronger player than you think, we need you." "Okay, fine."

It was not fine.

After one semester with a new symphony director, who was really nice and picked out the best music, I could not take it anymore. We began to have skills tests for which I could not find the time to prepare, and I had a huge fear of playing by myself, which was a result of having zero confidence in my skills. The thought of every wrong note being amplified and completely unhidden was nerve racking. Maybe it was the perfectionist coming out in me. The old director told me I was better than I thought I was. He would know because he saw me playing in the symphony, as well as my first audition, which was the hardest I've ever played. I practiced for that audition for three months.

But there was a day that I realized it was the end for me. I just knew I didn't belong anymore. However, I had a valid reason to end it. It came down to my late-night lab classes clashing with rehearsal times. It was hard for me to choose between the only fine arts I had left in my life, and the reason I was at Millikin. I went there to get a degree in Biology, and I was not leaving without it. The conflict in schedule made the choice for me. I wish I could have made that choice myself, but I guess it was the push I needed to move on from music and focus on what matters most, my degree. So the time had come to make the change happen. I remember sitting on the couch in the exec room of the sorority house, a nervous and sad wreck. Quitting and disappointing people are the two things in my life I actively avoid.

After a long phone call with the director of the symphony, and multiple emails with the registrar, I told the director of the symphony there was nothing more I was willing to do for this orchestra, since I did not want to be there anyway.

I felt like the oldest son at the end of Old Yeller.

His response?

"Keep on practicing. You will need to re-audition for the following semester." I always wondered if he knew I was not coming back.

The last concert pieces I played were Johannes Brahms' "Hungarian Dance No. 1," "Joyful Symphony No. 2," and "Cello Concerto in B-minor" by Antonin Dvorak. I believe the irony in this is that in high school we also played the "Hungarian Dances." I do not remember the exact piece numbers we played, but I was very excited to be playing these pieces. The "Hungarian Dances" are upbeat, fast, and loud, which is the kind of music that I lived for playing. To say the least, the concert was fun, and I felt as though I did not miss a beat. The bursts of rosin flew from my bow as it would hit the string, and my fingers danced across the neck of my instrument. I felt that passion I had forgotten about. Before I knew it, the concert was over. We were done. But, most importantly, I was done.

As I looked over my stand, I saw a large crowd through the stage lights and I felt nothing, knowing very well that this was probably the last concert I would ever play. I grabbed my music off the stand and walked off stage. I found my violin case, the one I begged for because it was so fancy, and I placed the instrument that I was so excited to pick out back in the red velvet lined case. I loosened the bow one last time before clicking it into its place. Click. Zip. It's over.

> The music folder
> Dropped in the bin
> The violin case
> Slung over my shoulder
> The Heels
> In my hand
> I walked out the door No
> remorse.

References

Matthews, M. (2011, August 28). *18 benefits of playing a musical instrument.* Retrieved from https://www.effectivemusicteaching.com/articles/directors/18-benefits-of-playing-a-musicalinstrument/

Merriam-Webster. (n.d.). *String instruments.* Retrieved from https://www.merriam-webster.com/dictionary/string/instruments

Payscale. (n.d.). Musician or singer salary. *Payscale.* Retrieved from https://www.payscale.com/research/US/Job=Musician_or_Singer/Salary

Pergola, J. (2014, February). *Music education in crisis.* NEMC. Retrieved from https://www.nemc.com/resources/articles/music-education-in-crisis_90

Snowdon, G. (2008, August 8). Pitch perfect. *The Guardian.* Retrieved from https://www.theguardian.com/money/2088/aug/09/workandcareers3

CHAPTER 43

The Eulogy

Sandra Brown

I knew you, Rejection, before I was born.
Had big sister been big brother,
I wouldn't be.
So strong the bond between you and me
that between become unseen.
Your names gave you me
and I took them.
I was you
every time I tried to prove my life
instead of live it.
I laughed when
we poured my pain in glasses
just so I couldn't feel
my soul break
again, and again, and again…
You scared me into getting it,
but you got me through it.
I feigned flawlessness flawlessly
in the name of names not mine.
And so I give yours back
I make mistakes.
Mistake is not my name.
Rejected, but that, too
is not my name.
As I bury you, Rejection,
I will honor your memory
by living that lesson,
honoring my thoughts,
embracing my emotions,
and loving my Self.

© KONINKLIJKE BRILL NV, LEIDEN, 2020 | DOI: 10.1163/9789004441651_044

CHAPTER 44

Yoga Me Free

Cara Quiett

In this flimsy cage,
The walls flutter away.
As my ribcage contracts and expands.

Society, let go of my hand,
Only for a brief while.

I slink down into child.
Dirt in my face but I'm
Cleansing my mind.

Trying to wipe the slate.
Deep breath in...
ERASE
EXHALE
ESCAPE

Dipping into cobra,
A graceful snake.
The bricks are marshmallows
Melting into the ground.
While my free spirit floats above this town.

This untethering keeps me together.
When the nested wires shred me apart.

© KONINKLIJKE BRILL NV, LEIDEN, 2020 | DOI: 10.1163/9789004441651_045

CHAPTER 45

Metamorphosis

Sandra Brown

My soul rejoices at
Making new choices;
At smiling new smiles,
Overcoming new trials.
It welcomes the thought
Of taking new chances,
Pursuing new dreams
And new circumstances.
Time to stop letting
The grip of old fears
Of loving gone years
Create new tears.
Time to let go
Of old hurts
Old pains—
New times for new
interests,
New dealings
New gains.

Old cries
Let die—
Life's highs
Let fly.
Don't sigh—
Forget why
Let yesteryear lie.

—Goodbye.

© KONINKLIJKE BRILL NV, LEIDEN, 2020 | DOI: 10.1163/9789004441651_046

Epilogue

Carmella J. Braniger, Rebekah M. Icenesse, Kathryn A. Coffey and Alex V. Miller

In this epilogue we wish to spotlight Shakespeare Corrected, an arts-outreach program that places undergraduate students together with incarcerated and disadvantaged populations in order to produce a theatrical experience that inspires transformation and fosters redemption in students, participants, and their families. In 2001, Millikin University Associate Professor of Theatre and Dance, Alex V. Miller, brought the "Shakespeare Corrected" Program to Decatur Correctional Center, a female facility.

The annual nine-month collaborative process over the past seven years has resulted in fully mounted Shakespeare productions. During the process, students and incarcerated become colleagues. Rehearsals become organic exchanges of ideas and life experiences, transcending anything that can be accomplished in the traditional classroom. While participating in the Shakespeare Corrected program, students and the incarcerated develop greater life-skills and intangibles such as respect, honesty, trust, humility, sharing, inclusivity, empathy, courage, forgiveness, and love. These ten tenants are the Essential Values of Peacemaking Circles developed by Kay Pranis, Barry Stuart, and Mark Wedge. Millikin students have the opportunity, while watching the prisoners delve into the universal human themes contained within Shakespeare's works, to challenge their own previously held beliefs about those incarcerated. In addition, public performances allow loved ones to view their mothers, daughters, sisters, and wives through a positive lens.

Evidence of the program's effectiveness is both qualitative and quantitative. Inmate Tiffany Wendel reflects: "It's something to show that I am doing something positive during my time here… so when we can get out, I can be a better mother to my children and a more functional citizen." Inmate Theresa Wright said her involvement in the program gave her new insights about her relationships with others: "If I communicate with Veronica in a negative way, she's going to respond to me in a negative way. It's about learning to better myself—for self-improvement. I don't want to go out of here the same way I came in here." Millikin student Rachel Reininger wrote in a reflection assignment, "Shakespeare Corrected changed my life." Janine Norman stated in a video testimonial that "When looking back at my Millikin experience, I have to say that this is the program that changed my life."

© KONINKLIJKE BRILL NV, LEIDEN, 2020 | DOI: 10.1163/9789004441651_047

Beyond testimonials, Shakespeare Corrected boasts a recidivism figure of 5%. This statistic takes on greater significance when held in comparison to the national average of 56.7%, the Illinois average of 48%, and the Decatur Correctional Center average of 20%. Last year, Shakespeare Corrected served 36 prisoners at a cost of $130.00 per offender. The state of Illinois pays $28,069 a year per inmate at Decatur Correctional. The monetary impact Shakespeare Corrected has upon the state of Illinois is great.

In addition to the Decatur Correctional Center, Shakespeare Corrected conducts work with Old King's Orchard Community Center, The Boys and Girls Club of Decatur, Milligan and Phoenix Academy/Alternative School, and Macon Resources Inc. for the developmentally challenged. These experiences affect all involved equally, as students enter various worlds and meet individuals beyond their typical sphere, shattering stereotypes and preconceived notions many of them unknowingly hold as truth.

Shakespeare Corrected[1] provides an inclusive, collaborative, and positive experience for well over 100 individuals of various needs, ages, and backgrounds every year. It is a transformative program that "enhances student awareness, understanding, and competence in dealing with diversity," and is an ideal example of democratic citizenship in a global environment.

Note

1   To learn more about Shakespeare Corrected, please visit https://www.millikin.edu/shakespeare-corrected

www.ingramcontent.com/pod-product-compliance
Lightning Source LLC
Chambersburg PA
CBHW050707280326
41926CB00088B/2863